INTRODUCTI

This Portuguese grammar has been written to meet the new demands of language teaching in schools and colleges and is particularly suitable for exam revision. The essential rules of the Portuguese language have been set in terms that are as accessible as possible to all users. Where technical terms have been used, then full explanations of these terms have also been supplied. There is also a full glossary of grammatical terminology on pages 7-18. While literary aspects of the Portuguese language have not been ignored, the emphasis has been placed squarely on modern spoken Portuguese. European Portuguese is the standard form used in this book but where significant differences exist for Brazilian Portuguese, these have been indicated. This grammar, with its wealth of lively and typical illustrations of usage taken from the present-day language, is the ideal study tool for all levels – from the beginner who is starting to come to grips with Portuguese through to the advanced user who requires a comprehensive and readily accessible work of reference.

Abbreviations used in the text:

[BP] Brazilian Portuguese
[EP] European Portuguese
f feminine
m masculine
pl plural
sing singular

CONTENTS

1. GLOSSARY OF GRAMMATICAL TERMS

ACCENTS

These are written marks above letters which affect either how that letter is pronounced, or at what point the word should be stressed (emphasised) when spoken. An accent can also be used to differentiate between two words with identical spellings but with different meanings. English does not use written accents (apart from on foreign words imported into the language), but many other languages do, including Portuguese. *Eg Pêra/avó/àquele.*

ACTIVE VOICE

The active form of a verb is the basic form, with Subject/ Verb/Object, as in *She bought the house,* as opposed to the passive form of the verb, as in *The house was bought by her.*

ADJECTIVES

Words which describe, or give more information about nouns. In Portuguese adjectives match their endings to the nouns they are linked with (eg if they are singular/plural or masculine/feminine). *Eg a pretty girl/those expensive coats.*

ADVERBS

These are words which describe, or tell us more about how an action (verb) is being carried out. They often answer the question How? They are also used to describe adjectives more fully, and you can use two adverbs together too. Often in English, an adverb has the ending '-ly' on it, and in Portuguese it may have '-mente'. *Eg He speaks loudly./They ran incredibly quickly.*

AGREEMENT

This is when related words have the same endings, according to number and gender, eg nouns and adjectives.

ANTECEDENT

The antecedent of a relative pronoun is the word or words to which the pronoun refers back. The antecedent is usually directly before the relative pronoun in a sentence, *eg I know the lady who made this, the lady* is the antecedent of '*who*'.

APPOSITION

A word or phrase is said to be in apposition to another when it is placed directly after it, with no other joining words, usually only commas, and gives more information about the original word/s, *eg John, our son, ...*

ARTICLES

Words which go with nouns. **Definite articles** are the words for 'the', and **indefinite articles** are the words for 'a/an/some'. In Portuguese there are different words corresponding to the number and gender (masculine/feminine).

AUGMENTATIVE

These are usually endings known as **suffixes**, added to nouns, to make them bigger, or more important, *eg porta (door) – portão (gate)*.

AUXILIARY VERB

These are verbs used in conjunction with another verb to form a different tense or the **passive voice**. The main auxiliary verbs in Portuguese are **ter** (to have) and **ser/estar** (to be), *eg She has been ill this week.*

CARDINAL NUMBERS

Numbers *one, two, three etc* (*um, dois, três...*).

CLAUSE

A group of words, which also contains a verb, *eg before we go out.../she swam well...*

COLLOQUIAL

This is a more casual, familiar style of spoken language.

COMPARATIVE

These are forms of adjectives and adverbs used to make comparisons, *eg thinner/more quickly.*

COMPOUND NOUN

These are nouns made up of two or more separate words. English examples include: *dinner party, shopping basket.*

COMPOUND TENSE

Compound tenses are verb tenses made up of more than one verb form, *eg he had gone/we will have seen (tinha ido/ teremos visto).*

CONJUGATE

This is what you do to a verb when you change its endings to denote person and tense, *eg We write/She writes/I wrote.*

CONJUGATION

The conjugation of a verb is the set of different endings changed as above. All regular verbs in Portuguese belong to one of three groups, or conjugations, of verbs that share a pattern for endings – those ending in **-ar**, **-er** and **-ir**.

CONJUNCTION

These are words which are used to join together other words, phrases or clauses, *eg and/but/because.*

COUNTABLE NOUN

A noun is said to be countable if it can form a plural, and be used with the indefinite article (a/some), *eg table/train/shirt*.

DEFINITE ARTICLE

The definite article is 'the' in English. In Portuguese there are four possibilities, depending on number and gender: *o/a/os/as.*

DEMONSTRATIVES

These are the words used for pointing things out – *this (one)/that (one)/these/those.*

DETERMINER

This is the term for words which can precede a noun, such as articles (definite and indefinite), possessives and demonstratives.

DIMINUTIVE

A diminutive ending is added to a noun or adjective to indicate smallness, cuteness, affection, and is very common in Portuguese, *eg mesa (table)/mesinha (small table)*.

DIRECT OBJECT

A direct object directly receives the action of a verb, as in: *I saw him/we're buying fish.* To determine whether an object is direct or indirect, ask the question 'what/whom?'. The direct object can directly answer it – *I saw whom? I saw him*.

DIRECT SPEECH

These are the exact words someone has spoken, usually contained within speech marks, and used with expressions such as *she said.../I replied...*

ELISION

Strictly speaking, elision is when the last letter of certain words is dropped, and an apostrophe inserted before the following word commencing with a vowel/silent h. This is only seen in a few place names in Portuguese (*eg Vila Praia d'Âncora)*, as otherwise the apostrophe is not used. However, what does happen in the spoken language is that words are run together so that they may appear to elide, *eg um copo de água (a glass of water)* may sound like *um copo d'água*.

ENDING

The endings of verbs are determined by the person carrying out the action *(I, you, he, she, it, we, they)*, the tense (past, present or future), and the **mood**. In Portuguese there are more verb endings than in English. Endings of words such as nouns and adjectives indicate number and gender.

EXCLAMATION

An exclamation is a word, phrase or sentence used to express surprise, annoyance, etc, *eg what!, what a pain!, how pretty!*

FEMININE

See Gender.

GENDER

The gender of a noun is whether it is masculine or feminine. All nouns in Portuguese fall into one or the other category, mostly without rhyme or reason, although more obvious ones relate to male and female people, animals and jobs. Adjectives in Portuguese also have gender, as they have to match the noun they are describing.

GERUND

The gerund (also known as the present participle) is the equivalent to the English part of the verb ending in '-ing', *eg speaking, drinking, reading.*

IDIOM/IDIOMATIC

These are expressions which are not easily directly translated into another language, and often not relating to normal rules of grammar, *eg to rain cats and dogs (chover a cântaros* – literally *to rain water jugs).*

IMPERATIVE

This is a form of verbs, known as a **mood**, used when giving commands or making suggestions, *eg stop!, don't do that!, let's go to the beach!*

IMPERSONAL VERB

This is a verb where the form used is usually in the 'it' form, *eg It is raining.*

INDEFINITE

Indefinite pronouns and adjectives are words which do not refer to a specific person or object, *eg someone, something.*

INDEFINITE ARTICLE

The indefinite article is the word for *a/an (some)*. In Portuguese, as with the definite article, there is a choice of four: *um/uma/uns/umas.*

INDICATIVE MOOD

This is the normal form of verbs used for straightforward statements, questions and negatives, as opposed to the **subjunctive mood** and **imperative**.

INDIRECT OBJECT

An indirect object is a noun or pronoun following a verb, and indirectly linked to that verb, usually by a preposition, often 'to' or 'for', although in English this is not always expressed, *eg I gave (to) her the book*.

INDIRECT SPEECH

Indirect speech is reported speech, or speech where the exact words of the original statements may not necessarily be used, and where speech marks are not required, *eg He said that he would not do it*.

INFINITIVE

This is the part of the verb referred to in English as 'TO...', and the form found in the dictionary before you change any of its endings, *eg to work/to run/to leave (trabalhar/correr/partir)*.

INFLECTION

This is the process of changes to the form of words (nouns, adjectives, etc), to denote person, number, tense, mood or voice.

INTERROGATIVES

Question forms, *eg Where?/Which?/How?*

MASCULINE

See Gender.

MODAL AUXILIARIES

Modals are verbs used in conjunction with another verb in order to express a 'mood', such as wanting, liking, obligation, ability and possibility, *eg I would like to go home./Could you take me?*

MOOD

Verbs are divided into three usage groups, each of which uses its own particular endings across a range of tenses: indicative (expressing fact), subjunctive (non-factual or contrary to fact), and imperative (commands).

NEGATIVE

Negatives express ideas such as *no, never, no-one etc.*

NOUNS

A noun is any thing, person or abstract idea in existence – everything around us is a noun of some kind. A noun can be singular (just one), or plural (more than one). In Portuguese nouns are also divided into masculine and feminine words, *eg table/horses/man-men/happiness.*

NUMBER

This refers to whether a word is singular (just one) or plural (more than one).

OBJECT

The person or thing on the receiving end of the action of a verb. Objects can be 'direct' – *ie* they directly receive the action of the verb, or 'indirect' – where they receive the results of the action, through indirect means. *Eg She gives money every week* (*money* is a direct object)/*She gives them money every week* (*them* is an indirect object).

ORDINAL NUMBERS

First, second, third, etc (primeiro, segundo, terceiro.).

PASSIVE VOICE

A verb can be used in the passive voice, when the subject of the verb does not carry out the action, but is subjected to it. It is often formed with a part of the verb *to be (ser)* and the past participle, *eg the window was broken by the boys.*

PAST PARTICIPLE

Together with an auxiliary verb, the past participle forms certain compound tenses (tenses made up from two different verbs). They are also used in the **passive voice**, and as adjectives, *eg I had broken the window/The window was broken/It's a broken window (Tinha partido a janela/A janela foi partida/É uma janela partida)*.

PERSON

Each verb has three persons in the singular (1st – I/2nd – you/3rd – he/she/it), and three in the plural (1st – we/2nd – you/3rd – they). In Portuguese, polite forms of 'you' (*eg você/o senhor/as senhoras*) are also connected to the 3rd person singular and plural of the verb.

PERSONAL PRONOUNS

Personal pronouns take the place of a noun. They usually accompany a verb and can either be the subject (*I, you, we, etc*) or an object of the verb (*me, him, us, etc*). They are commonly used with prepositions, and can also be **reflexive**.

PHRASE

A phrase is a group of words which together have some meaning, *eg in the garden, after midnight*.

PLURAL

See Number.

POSSESSIVES

These are words denoting possession or ownership. They can be adjectives or pronouns, which in Portuguese means there is a choice of four different words for each possessive, depending on number and gender, *eg my/our/his*.

PREFIX

A letter or letters which can be added to the beginning of a word in order to change its basic meaning in some way, *eg possible – impossible.*

PREPOSITIONS

These are words which denote the 'position' of someone or something in time or place. *Eg on top of the cupboard/before going out/at six o'clock.*

PRESENT PARTICIPLE

This form, also known as the **gerund**, corresponds to the English '-ing' form, *eg swimming, running, departing (nadando, correndo, partindo),* although in Portuguese it may be used in different ways.

PRONOUNS

These are words which take the place of a noun (pro = for), so that you do not need to keep repeating the actual noun itself each time you want to refer to it. *Eg Mary is very kind. She looks after my cat. She gives it lots of food.*

QUESTIONS

There are two forms of question: direct questions stand on their own and require a question mark at the end, *eg when will he arrive?;* indirect questions are introduced by a clause and require no question mark – these are often used in indirect speech, *eg I asked when he would come.*

REFLEXIVE VERBS

Actions with a bearing on the subject of the verb – the action is carried out by, and also on, the subject, *ie* they reflect back to the person carrying out the action. Reflexive verbs carry the word 'self' with them, although it is not always expressed in English. *Eg Enjoy yourselves!/She gets herself dressed each morning.*

SENTENCE

A group of words, with a beginning, an end, and a finite verb, which has a meaning. A sentence may have any number of separate clauses, but one of these will be the main clause, which can make sense in its own right as a sentence. *Eg She wants to visit Spain./If we buy the house, we cannot have a holiday too.*

SIMPLE TENSE

A simple tense is one in which the verb form consists of only one word, unlike a compound tense, *eg falo, veremos, fomos.*

SINGULAR

See Number.

STEM

The stem is the part of a verb to which you add the endings to show person and tense. In Portuguese the stem is found by first removing the **–ar**/**-er**/**-ir** from the infinitive of the verb. Some irregular verbs may have a different stem.

SUBJECT

The person or thing carrying out the action of a verb, *eg My brother wants to be an engineer./Our dog sleeps a lot.*

SUBJUNCTIVE MOOD

This is a separate set of verb endings for use in certain situations, such as in 'if' clauses, or with expressions of doubt, *eg If I were rich... (se eu for rica...).*

SUFFIX

This is a letter or letters which can be added to the end of a word to change its basic meaning, or the type of word it is, *eg sad – sadness.* Portuguese uses these quite a lot.

SUPERLATIVE

This is the form of an adjective or adverb denoting the highest or lowest level, *eg the fastest car/the most expensive shoes.*

SYLLABLE

This is a part of a word containing one, two or more letters which together divide up each word as we say it, *eg ta-ble/ po-ta-to (me-sa/ba-ta-ta).*

TAG QUESTION

These are short question-expressions which, when 'tagged' on to the end of a sentence, turn it into a question, *eg It's turned out nice, hasn't it?*

TENSES

These are the time references for when verbs are taking place. There are different tenses in the present, past and future.

VERBS

Verbs convey actions or state of being, or sometimes an abstract state. Verbs have an 'infinitive' form, which tells you the name of the verb itself, but no other information, and relates to the English 'TO do something'. A sentence must have a verb in a 'finite' form – which tells you what the action is, who is doing it, and at what point in time (in the past, present or future). *Eg She goes home by train/I read the paper today.*

VOICE

The two voice forms of a verb are **active** and **passive**.

2. ARTICLES

A. THE DEFINITE ARTICLE

1. Forms

In English, there is only one form of the definite article: **the**. In Portuguese there are four forms, depending on the gender and the number of the noun following the article:

	Singular	Plural
masculine	**o**	**os**
feminine	**a**	**as**

2. Forms with prepositions

The definite article combines with a number of prepositions, and results in the following contracted forms:

a) with **a** (to, at)

a +	**o**	**a**	**os**	**as**
	= **ao**	= **à**	= **aos**	= **às**

ao cinema
to/at the cinema

à praia
to/at the beach

aos alunos
to the pupils

às lojas
to the shops

b) with **de** (of, from)

de +	**o**	**a**	**os**	**as**
	= **do**	= **da**	= **dos**	= **das**

do médico
of/from the doctor

da região
of/from the region

dos professores
of/from the teachers

das ilhas
of/from the islands

c) with **por** (by, for, through)

por +	**o**	**a**	**os**	**as**
	= **pelo**	= **pela**	= **pelos**	= **pelas**

pelo parque
through/by the park

pela praça
through/by the square

pelos políticos
by the politicians

pelas ondas
through the waves

d) with **em** (in/on)

em +	**o**	**a**	**os**	**as**
	= **no**	= **na**	= **nos**	= **nas**

no rio
in the river

na casa
in the house

nos jornais
in the papers

nas árvores
in/on the trees

3. Use

As in English, the definite article is used when referring to something known or given:

as casas naquela rua
the houses in that street

o bolo está seco
the cake is dry

However, the definite article is used far more frequently in Portuguese than in English, in particular in the following cases:

a) with titles, first names and some forms of address

posso apresentar o senhor engenheiro José Neto
may I introduce (Engineer) José Neto

o João mora em Cascais
João lives in Cascais

a dona Rita está boa?
are you well, (Dona) Rita?

b) with continents, countries (although not all, including Portugal itself), and provinces

a Europa tem muitos países
Europe has many countries

queremos visitar o Brasil
we want to visit Brazil

o Algarve é uma região turística
the Algarve is a tourist region

c) with names of towns which also have a real meaning (although this is not totally consistent)

tem um apartamento na Figueira da Foz
he has a flat in Figueira da Foz (lit. the fig tree of the river mouth)

but: **Lagos fica no Algarve**
Lagos (lit. Lakes) is in the Algarve

d) with parts of the body, as a substitute for the possessive adjectives

vou lavar as mãos
I'm going to wash my hands

cortou o dedo
he cut his finger

e) with articles of clothing, as a substitute for the possessive adjectives

dei o casaco ao meu amigo
I gave my coat to my friend

vamos pôr as luvas antes de sairmos?
shall we put on our gloves before we go out?

f) with nouns used in a general sense

as pessoas em geral gastam muito dinheiro
people in general spend a lot of money

os cigarros fazem mal à saúde
cigarettes are bad for the health

g) with units of measurement

as pêras custam 2 euros o quilo
(the) pears cost 2 euros a kilo

isto é uma pechincha – só 3 euros a garrafa
this is a bargain – just 3 euros a bottle

h) with names of meals

vão tomar o pequeno almoço ao café
they're going to have breakfast at the café

queres ficar para o jantar?
do you want to stay for dinner?

i) with certain public institutions

ficou dois anos na cadeia
she spent two years in jail

quero estudar história na universidade
I want to study History at university

j) with the names of languages

o português é uma língua importante
Portuguese is an important language

ela adora o japonês
she loves Japanese

But: the definite article is not used with languages after **de** or **em**, and not always used after the verbs **aprender**, **ensinar**, **entender**, **estudar**, **falar** and **saber**.

nunca aprendi italiano
I have never learnt Italian

entendemos um pouco de francês
we understand a bit of French

k) with the possessive adjectives and pronouns

este é o meu filho
this is my son

as tuas amigas moram perto
your friends live nearby

l) with days of the week

o filme termina no domingo
the film finishes on Sunday

m) with seas, rivers, mountains and constellations

o oceano Pacífico	the Pacific Ocean
o mar Morto	the Dead Sea
o (rio) Tejo	the (river) Tagus
os Pirineus	the Pyrenees
a Via-Láctea	the Milky Way

n) before the names of musical notes

o fá, o lá, o mi etc.

o) before names of sporting clubs

o Benfica
o Sporting
o Botafogo [Brazil]

gosto muito do Benfica
I like Benfica a lot

p) before seasons

a Primavera spring	**o Outono** autumn
o Verão summer	**o Inverno** winter

sempre tiro férias na Primavera
I always have my holidays in spring

4. Omission of the definite article

The definite article is not used in the following situations:

a) with numerals used with the name of a ruler

Carlos V (quinto)
Charles the Fifth

Maria II (segunda)
Mary the Second

b) with nouns used 'in apposition' (*ie* two nouns following each other, referring to the same person, place or thing)

este é Alberto Máximo, rei da ilha
this is Albert Maximus, (the) king of the island

c) before the word **casa** (house), when it refers to 'home'

vou para casa
I'm going home

ela não está em casa
she is not at home

d) with many sayings and proverbs

Setembro molhado, figo estragado
wet September, ruined fig

em Agosto, sardinhas e mosto
in August, sardines and wine must

e) with months

Janeiro é o meu mês preferido
January is my favourite month

ela faz anos em Julho
it's her birthday in July

5. Repetition of the definite article

The definite article is repeated in the following situations:

a) when the terms used are opposites

o dia e a noite
day and night

o bem e o mal
good and bad

a vida e a morte
life and death

b) when there is reference to different people or things

o Presidente e o Primeiro Ministro participaram
the President and the Prime Minister took part

a opinião da Clara e a (opinião) do Paulo
Clara and Paulo's opinion

B. THE INDEFINITE ARTICLE

1. Forms

The forms of the indefinite article (a, an, some) are the same as the number one in the singular, but also have a masculine and feminine plural:

	Singular	Plural
masculine	**um**	**uns**
feminine	**uma**	**umas**

um chá
a tea

uma saia
a skirt

uns sapatos
some shoes

umas bananas
some bananas

2. Use

On the whole, the indefinite article is used in the same way as in English:

um livro sobre Lisboa
a book about Lisbon

umas pessoas simpáticas
some nice people

3. Omission of the indefinite article

The indefinite article is not used in the following situations:

a) With nouns expressing rank

ela é gerente da Ford
she is a manager with Ford

o meu tio era capitão
my uncle was a captain

b) When expressing professions or occupations

sou professora
I am a teacher

o Pedro era piloto
Pedro used to be a pilot

c) With nouns in apposition

Lisboa, cidade antiga e cultural
Lisbon, an old, cultural city

o Nuno, jogador com Benfica
Nuno, a player with Benfica

d) Often with words such as: **cem, mil, que!, certo, meio, outro**

custou cem libras
it cost a hundred pounds

que bebé bonito!
what a beautiful baby!

e) Often when expressing shopping items

vou comprar pão
I'm going to buy some bread

precisamos de manteiga
we need some butter

vamos comprar cerejas?
shall we buy some cherries?

C. THE NEUTER ARTICLE

The neuter article is not attached to masculine or feminine nouns, but is used with a masculine, singular adjective to express an abstract or general quality of the adjective. In English we often use the word 'thing' with an adjective in the same way.

para mim, o importante era chegar a tempo
for me, the important thing (what was important) was arriving on time

o curioso é que ninguém mora lá
the curious thing is that no one lives there

3. NOUNS

A noun is a word or group of words which refers to a person, an animal, a thing, a place or an abstract idea.

A. GENDER

a) All nouns in Portuguese are grouped into either masculine or feminine words. The so-called 'gender' of words denoting people or animals is determined by their obvious sex.

o senhor gentleman/sir	**a senhora** lady/madam
o pai father	**a mãe** mother
o galo cockerel	**a galinha** hen

b) Usually, words ending in **-o** are masculine, and those ending in **-a** are feminine.

o quadro picture	**a mesa** table
o carro car	**a cadeira** chair
o livro book	**a camisa** shirt

B. FORMATION OF FEMININES

a) Many nouns become feminine by changing the final **-o** to **-a**, or by adding **-a** to the existing masculine form.

o amigo (male) friend	**a amig*a*** (female) friend
o tio uncle	**a ti*a*** aunt
o pintor (male) painter	**a pintor*a*** (female) painter

b) However, not all nouns fit comfortably into these categories. Some words end in **-a** but are, in fact, masculine, and some ending in **-o** are feminine.

o mapa map	**o telegrama** telegram

o guia guidebook — **o dia** day
a mão hand — **a avó** grandmother

c) Nouns ending in **-l** and **-r** are generally masculine, while those ending with the letters **-ade**, **-ção** and **-gem** are generally feminine.

o jornal newspaper
o sabor flavour
a universidade university
a informação information
a garagem garage

As gender is not always obvious from the ending of a word, nouns should be learned together with the appropriate article.

C. FORMATION OF PLURALS

a) The plural (*ie* when there is more than one) of nouns ending in a vowel is formed by simply adding **-s**.

a caneta pen — **as caneta*s*** pens
o sapato shoe — **os sapato*s*** shoes
a árvore tree — **as árvore*s*** trees

b) The plural of nouns ending in a consonant other than **-l** or **-m** is formed by adding **-es**.

a flor flower — **as flor*es*** flowers
o rapaz boy — **os rapaz*es*** boys

c) Words ending in **-m** form their plural by changing the **-m** to **-ns**.

o jardim garden — **os jardi*ns*** gardens
a estalagem inn — **as estalage*ns*** inns

d) Words ending in **-l** change the **-l** to **-is**. If the word ends in **-il**, this changes to **-is** if the final syllable is stressed, but changes to **-eis** if the syllable is unstressed. Words ending in **-el** take an acute accent on the **e** (**é**) if the final syllable is stressed. The same happens on the **o** of words ending in **-ol.**

o jornal newspaper	**os jorna*is*** newspapers
o pastel pastry/tart	**os pasté*is*** pastries
o ardil trick/ruse	**os ard*is*** tricks/ruses
o réptil reptile	**os répt*eis*** reptiles
o espanhol Spaniard/ Spanish	**os espanhó*is*** Spaniards

e) Words ending in **-ão** either add a final **-s** or change to **-ões** or **-ães**; there is no standard rule.

a mão hand	**as m*ãos*** hands
a questão question	**as quest*ões*** questions
o cão dog	**os c*ães*** dogs

f) The masculine plural form is used to denote a combination of two or more masculine and feminine people.

o amigo friend (male)	**os amigos** friends
o pai father	**os pais** parents
o tio uncle	**os tios** uncles/uncles and aunts
o sobrinho nephew	**os sobrinhos** nephews/ nephews and nieces

D. ABSTRACT NOUNS

Abstract nouns, formed with or followed by an adjective, are neuter and have no masculine or feminine gender, and therefore do not change in any way.

o importante the important thing/what is important...
o interessante the interesting thing/what's interesting...
o difícil the difficult thing/what's difficult...

4. ADJECTIVES

A. AGREEMENT

Adjectives are words that describe, or give additional information about, nouns and pronouns. They agree with the noun in number and gender. If an adjective describes two or more nouns of different gender, then it is placed in the masculine plural.

o vestido preto
the black dress

a camisa amarela
the yellow shirt

os sapatos caros
the expensive shoes

as cadeiras baratas
the cheap chairs

o restaurante é moderno
the restaurant is modern

a praia é bonita
the beach is pretty

os homens são velhos
the men are old

as janelas são novas
the windows are new

o Pedro e a Ana são americanos
Peter and Anne are American

B. GENDER

Like nouns, adjectives are masculine or feminine, depending on the noun they are describing.

a) Those ending in **-o** switch to a final **-a** in the feminine.

o casaco curto
the short coat

a saia curta
the short skirt

b) If an adjective ends in **-e** or a consonant, the masculine and feminine forms are usually identical.

o touro contente the happy bull	**a vaca contente** the happy cow
o livro difícil the difficult book	**a lição difícil** the difficult lesson

c) Adjectives of nationality do not always follow this rule.

o vinho espanhol the Spanish wine	**a música espanhola** the Spanish music

d) Other masculine–feminine changes include:

	MASCULINE			FEMININE
-or	**sofredor**	suffering	+ **a**	**sofredor*a***
-ês	**português**	Portuguese	+ **a**	**portugues*a***
-u	**cru**	raw	+ **a**	**cru*a***
-eu	**europeu**	European	+ **eia**	**europe*ia****
-ão	**alemão**	German	+ **ã**	**alem*ã***

***[BP européia]**

There are many exceptions to the above-stated rules, which you pick up as you go along.

C. PLURALS

a) In general, the plurals of adjectives are formed according to the same rules as for nouns.

o professor velho the old teacher	**os sapatos velhos** the old shoes
a ovelha infeliz the unhappy sheep	**as meninas infelizes** the unhappy girls
uma porta azul a blue door	**os olhos azuis** the blue eyes

b) i) with compound adjectives, it is the last part of the compound which becomes plural, provided that that word itself is an adjective:

acordos luso-brasileiros
Luso-Brazilian agreements

olhos verde-claros
light-green eyes

ii) if the last part of the compound is a noun, none of the compound becomes plural:

lenços amarelo-limão
lemon-yellow handkerchiefs

saias cor-de-rosa
pink skirts

iii) if a colour is indicated simply by the name of a fruit, item, animal or product, no plurals are made:

camisas limão
lemon shirts

calças vinho
wine(-coloured) trousers

iv) the compound colours **azul-marinho** (navy blue) and **azul-celeste** (sky blue) are invariable:

tenho três blusas azul-marinho
I have three navy-blue blouses

prefiro estas azul-celeste
I prefer these sky-blue ones

D. POSITION

Adjectives are usually placed *after* the noun they are describing, although they can also be found before the noun.

a) In some cases certain adjectives change their meaning slightly from the original when they change position.

uma senhora *pobre* a poor woman (in wealth)
uma *pobre* senhora a poor woman (pitiful)

Other adjectives which act in this way include:

	Before the Noun	After the Noun
grande	great	big
mesmo	same	self
vários	several	various
velho	old (long-standing)	old
certo	certain (some)	correct
caro	dear (cherished)	dear, expensive
único	single/only	unique

uma grande obra a great work	**uma camisa grande** a large shirt
a mesma coisa the same thing	**ele mesmo** he himself
vários vinhos several wines	**livros vários** various books
o meu velho amigo my old friend	**a casa velha** the old house
certas pessoas some/certain people	**a resposta certa** the correct reply
cara Maria Dear Maria	**um cinto caro** an expensive belt
a única maneira the only way	**uma oportunidade única** a unique opportunity

b) The following adjectives tend to be used more frequently before the noun, but can be used in either position:

bom	good	**mau**	bad
lindo	pretty	**próximo**	next
pequeno	small	**último**	last

este é um bom filme
this is a good film

a última sessão da tarde
the last session/showing of the afternoon (evening)

a que horas parte o próximo barco?
when does the next boat leave?

c) The cardinal numbers (**primeiro**, "first", **segundo**, "second", etc) are also normally placed before the noun.

é a primeira rua à direita
it's the first street on the right.

este é o terceiro livro Harry Potter
this is the third Harry Potter book.

E. SUFFIXES

a) Instead of using the word **muito** ("very") with an adjective, the suffix **-íssimo** can be added to the adjective instead. Adjectives ending in a vowel lose the vowel before the suffix is added.

caro	expensive	**caríssimo**	very expensive
pobre	poor	**pobríssimo**	very poor
inteligent	intelligent	**inteligent-íssimo**	very intelligent

os brincos são caríssimos
the earrings are really expensive

ela é inteligentíssima
she is very intelligent

A number of adjectives formed this way are irregular, and some have an alternative, 'erudite' ending of **-rimo**. Here is a selection:

ágil	agile	**agílimo**
agradável	pleasant	**agradabilíssimo**
benéfico	beneficial	**beneficentíssimo**
benévolo	benevolent	**benevolentíssimo**
capaz	capable	**capacíssimo**
célebre	famous	**celebérrimo**
difícil	difficult	**dificílimo**
doce	sweet	**dulcíssimo**
fácil	easy	**facílimo**
frágil	fragile	**fragílimo**
incrível	incredible	**incredibilíssimo**
livre	free	**libérrimo**
magnífico	magnificent	**magnificentíssimo**
nobre	noble	**nobilíssimo**
pobre	poor	**paupérrimo**
próspero	prosperous	**prospérrimo**
sábio	wise	**sapientíssimo**
simpático	pleasant	**simpaticíssimo**
terrível	terrible	**terribilíssimo**
voraz	greedy	**voracíssimo**

b) Another widely-used suffix, **-inho**, denotes affection, pity or simply a smaller size.

bonito	pretty	**bonitinho**	cute, really pretty
obrigado	thank you	**obrigadinho**	thanks a lot
coitado	poor, pitiful	**coitadinho**	poor little thing

These endings follow the general rules for plural and feminine forms. For other examples of suffixes see page 209.

c) Many adjectives have their origins in nouns, often coming from a Latin root. Examples include:

		From	
auditivo	hearing	**ouvido**	(inner) ear
áureo	golden	**ouro**	gold

auricular	hearing	**orelha**	ear
canino	canine	**cão**	dog
cardíaco	cardiac	**coração**	heart
diabólico	diabolical/devilish	**diabo**	devil
lácteo	milk(y)	**leite**	milk
linear	linear	**linha**	line
lunar	lunar	**lua**	moon
marginal	marginal	**margem**	bank, edge
nasal	nasal	**nariz**	nose
ocular	ocular	**olho**	eye
real	royal	**rei**	king
solar	solar	**sol**	sun
terrestre	terrestrial	**terra**	earth
vítreo	glass	**vidro**	glass

F. COMPARATIVES AND SUPERLATIVES

a) To form the comparative of an adjective, place **mais** ("more") or **menos** ("less") before it. To form the superlative, use the definite article with the comparative. Comparative and superlative adjectives must agree with the nouns they describe.

Adjective		Comparative		Superlative	
alto	tall	***mais*** **alto**	taller	***o mais*** **alto**	the tallest
feliz	happy	***mais*** **feliz**	happier	***o mais*** **feliz**	the happiest

o Pedro é alto; a Carmen é mais alta; o João é o mais alto
Pedro is tall; Carmen is taller; João is the tallest

eu estou feliz, mas ela está mais feliz
I am happy, but she is happier

b) Comparatives of inferiority also exist, but are used less:

menos caro less expensive (*ie* cheaper)
o menos caro the least expensive

c) In the superlative, if a noun is expressed, the definite article should go before it, and both the article and the noun appear before the superlative adjective.

o Rolex é o mais caro
the Rolex is the most expensive

o Rolex é *o relógio* mais caro
the Rolex is the most expensive watch

d) The article may be used with a possessive, which it precedes.

a Paula é a minha amiga mais chegada
Paula is my closest friend

e) **De** is used to translate "in" after a superlative, and not **em**.

é o carro mais rápido do mundo
it is the fastest car in the world

f) Some adjectives have irregular comparatives.

Adjective		Comparative		Superlative	
bom	good	***melhor***	better	***o melhor; óptimo****	best
mau	bad	***pior***	worse	***o pior; péssimo***	worst
grande	big	***maior*****	bigger	***o maior; máximo***	biggest
pequeno	small	***menor*****	smaller	***o menor; mínimo***	smallest

*** [BP ótimo]**
** You will also come across **mais grande** (on rare occasions) and **mais pequeno**

estou melhor
I am better

é o meu melhor amigo
he is my best friend

tem maior?
have you any larger?

o preço mínimo
the smallest price

g) Comparison of age

In Portuguese, **mais velho** ("older/oldest (eldest)") and **mais novo** ("younger/youngest") are used.

o meu irmão mais novo
my younger/youngest brother

ela é a mais nova da família
she is the youngest in the family

h) Levels of comparison

Nouns can be compared in a variety of ways. The word "than" can be expressed as **do que** or simply **que**.

i) Inequality

do que, que	than
mais... (do) que	more... than
menos... (do) que	less... than

o Nuno é mais alto do que o José
Nuno is taller than José

em Portugal está menos frio do que na Inglaterra
in Portugal it is less cold than in England

Do que (or just **que**) is also used when the clause following the comparison contains a verb:

nós compramos mais comida (do) que precisamos
we buy more food than we need

Mais de and **menos de** are used with quantities or numbers:

tenho menos de vinte euros
I have less than twenty euros

aprende francês há mais de cinco anos
she has been learning French for more than five years

ii) Equality

tão + adjective... **como/quanto**	as... as
tanto/a + noun... **como**	as much... as
tantos/as + noun... **como**	as many... as

este livro não é tão bom como aquele
this book is not as good as that one

não gastei tanto dinheiro como você
I didn't spend as much money as you

tenho tantos chocolates como você
I have as many chocolates as you

iii) Ratio

quanto mais... (tanto) mais	the more... the more
quanto mais... (tanto) menos	the more... the less
quanto menos... (tanto) mais	the less... the more
quanto menos... (tanto) menos	the less... the less

quanto mais caro for o hotel, (tanto) mais confortável o quarto
the more expensive the hotel, the more comfortable the room

quanto mais cansado, menos animado está
the more tired you are, the less cheerful

quanto menos bonito esteja o rapaz, (tanto) mais interessante
the less attractive a boy may be, the more interesting (he is)

quanto mais preocupado está, mais nervoso fica
the more worried you are, the more nervous you become

5. ADVERBS

Adverbs are words that provide information about verbs, adjectives and other adverbs. Many of them are equivalent to the English adjective + *-ly*.

A. FORMATION

a) Most adverbs are formed by adding **-mente** to the feminine singular of the adjective form. (If the adjective has only one form for both genders, that form is used.) Accents on the original adjective are dropped.

lento	slow	**lentamente**	slowly
rápido	fast	**rapidamente**	quickly
verdadeiro	true	**verdadeiramente**	truly
infeliz	unhappy	**infelizmente**	unhappily/ unfortunately

o caracol anda lentamente
the snail walks slowly

ela anda rapidamente
she walks quickly

ela está verdadeiramente feliz
she is truly happy

infelizmente, não posso ir
unfortunately I cannot go

b) If two or more adverbs are used in a series of descriptions, **-mente** should be placed only at the end of the last one.

ela fala rápido e fluentemente
she speaks quickly and fluently

B. AVOIDING THE USE OF -MENTE

a) To enhance style and avoid repetition, adverbs ending in **-mente** can be replaced by any of the following:

com + noun	(with...)
duma maneira + adjective	(in a... manner)
dum modo + adjective	(in a... way)

dificilmente	**com dificuldade**	with difficulty
agitadamente	**duma maneira agitada**	in an agitated manner
levemente	**dum modo leve**	in a light way

b) Adverbs which do not fall into the **-mente** group include:

devagar	slowly	**bem**	well
mal	badly	**cedo**	early
sempre	always/still	**depois**	afterwards/later
depressa	quickly		

fale mais devagar
speak more slowly

canta bem
he sings well

desenha mal
she draws badly

levanto-me cedo
I get up early

sempre compramos demais
we always buy too much

depois vamos ao teatro
we're going to the theatre later

a professora fala depressa
the teacher speaks quickly

c) Often Portuguese uses an adjective in the masculine singular when an adverb would be used in English.

você fala alto
you speak loudly

C. COMPARISON OF ADVERBS

a) Comparative adverbs are formed in the same way as comparative adjectives, by using **mais** or **menos**. The superlative also follows the same pattern as for adjectives.

a Sofia fala devagar
Sofia speaks slowly

a Ana fala mais devagar
Ana speaks more slowly

a Ana fala mais devagar do que a Sofia
Ana speaks more slowly than Sofia

a Carla fala a mais devagar
Carla speaks the slowest

b) **o mais... possível** as... as possible

o mais rápido possível
as quickly as possible

o mais paciente possível
as patiently as possible

c) Irregular comparisons

bem	well	**melhor**	better	**o melhor**	the best
mal	badly	**pior**	worse	**o pior**	the worst

eu trabalho melhor do que ele
I work better than him

você é o que trabalha o melhor da turma
you work the best in the class

corremos mal
we run badly

elas correm ainda pior
they run even worse

6. PRONOUNS

A. SUBJECT PRONOUNS

The subject of a verb is the person (or thing) carrying out the action, and can be represented by a pronoun in the first, second, or third person, singular or plural, as follows:

	Singular		Plural	
1st	I	**eu**	we	**nós**
2nd	you	**tu**	you	**vós**
3rd	he/it	**ele**	they *(m)*	**eles**
	she/it	**ela**	they *(f)*	**elas**
	you	**você**	You	**vocês**

Forms of address (how you call someone "you") can be complex, but in general:

tu	family, close friends, children, pets
você	predominant in Brazil, widely used in Portugal – slightly more formal
o/a + first name	colleagues, less-close friends
o senhor/a senhora	very polite, with strangers, older people
verb on its own*	verb in 3rd person singular
vós	"you" plural, mainly now just church services, when addressing crowds/some older people, especially in rural areas

vocês	widespread, acceptable form for "you" plural
os senhores/as senhoras	polite address
verb on its own*	verb in 3rd person plural

*neutral, polite form

Portuguese subject pronouns do not necessarily need to be used with the verb, as in many cases the verb ending denotes the subject. However, to avoid any ambiguity, pronouns should be used with the third person forms (which can mean he, she, it, they or you), unless there is no doubt as to who or what the subject is.

B. OBJECT PRONOUNS

Object pronouns receive the action of the verb. They can be direct, indirect or reflexive, and can be used with prepositions.

a) Direct object pronouns

The direct object directly receives the action of the verb. It responds to the direct questions What? or Whom?

Singular		Plural	
me	me	**nos**	us
te	you	**vos**	you
o *(m)*	him; it; you	**os** *(m)*	them; you
a *(f)*	her; it; you	**as** *(f)*	them; you

vejo-te
I see you

compraste-o?
did you buy it?

ajuda-nos
help us

In colloquial usage in Brazil, it is common practice for the pronouns **o/a/os/as** to be replaced by **ele/ela/eles/elas**.

você viu ela?
did you see her?

b) Changes to spelling following verbs

With direct object pronouns in the third person (**o, a, os, as**) certain changes occur in the following situations:

i) Following verb forms ending in **-r**, **-s**, and **-z**.

These final letters are omitted, and an **-l** is inserted before the pronoun. In the case of the omission of final **-r**, in **-ar** and **-er** (but not **-ir**) verbs the following written accents are added to the remaining final vowel, in order to maintain stress on the correct syllable:

-ar	**-á**
-er	**-ê**

Accents are also required on compounds of the verb **pôr** (to put), *eg* **pô-lo**, and on **faz** (make/do), **traz** (bring), and **fez** (did/made). The verb form **quer** (want) adds an 'e', in **quere-o** etc, and the forms **ten** (you have) becomes **tem-lo**, etc.

vou convidar a minha amiga: vou convidá-la
I'm going to invite my friend: I'm going to invite her

bebes o vinho, ou não? bebe-lo ou não?
are you drinking the wine or not? are you drinking it or not?

ela faz os bolos: ela fá-los
she makes the cakes: she makes them

ele quer os livros: ele quere-os
he wants the books: he wants them

tu tens a minha mala: tu tem-la
you have my bag: you have it

ii) Following verb forms ending in **-m**, **-ão**, and **-õe**, the endings are maintained, but an **n** is added before the pronoun.

Eles compram a casa. Eles compram-na.
They buy the house. They buy it.

Os amigos dão os presentes à Paula. Os amigos dãonos à Paula.
The friends give the presents to Paula. The friends give them to Paula.

Põe o livro na estante. Põe-no na estante.
Put the book on the bookcase. Put it on the bookcase.

c) Indirect object pronouns

The indirect object has an indirect relation to the action of the verb. It denotes the person or thing to or for whom the action is performed. You can test out whether an indirect object pronoun is required by asking yourself if you can add the word "to" (or "for") before the pronoun. It is worth doing this anyway, as in English we do not always use "to" or "for" in this type of sentence.

eg I gave the keys to him. (I gave him the keys)
I gave what? The keys = Direct Object.
To whom? To him = Indirect Object.

Singular		Plural	
me	to me	**nos**	to us
te	to you	**vos**	to you
lhe	to him, her, to it, you	**lhes**	to them, you

deu-me umas flores
He gave me some flowers

mando-lhe uma carta
I send a letter to him/her/you

d) To avoid ambiguity with the indirect object pronoun in the third person, the following constructions can be added:

a ele/ela/você/o senhor/a senhora

mando-lhe uma carta a ele
I send him a letter

Or even simply: **mando uma carta a ele**

C. REFLEXIVE PRONOUNS

A reflexive pronoun accompanies an appropriate reflexive verb and refers back to the subject of that verb. Reflexive verbs are indicated in the dictionary by **-se**, attached to the infinitive. Many non-reflexive verbs can also be made reflexive.

Singular		Plural	
me	myself	**nos**	ourselves
te	yourself	**vos**	yourselves
se	himself, herself, itself, yourself	**se**	themselves, yourselves

levanta-se às 7
he (she etc) gets up at 7 o'clock

como te chamas?
what are you called?

sentaram-se à mesa
they sat down at the table

The final **-s** of the first person plural verb form is dropped before the reflexive.

encontramo-nos no bar?
shall we meet in the bar?

D. POSITION OF OBJECT PRONOUNS

a) In Portugal, the object pronouns (direct, indirect or reflexive), are usually attached to the end of the verb by a hyphen. In Brazil, object pronouns are more often found preceding the verb in affirmative sentences, especially when a subject pronoun is expressed first.

they went to bed late
elas deitaram-se tarde [EP]
elas se deitaram tarde [BP]

I'm called Ronaldo
chamo-me Ronaldo [EP]
eu me chamo Ronaldo [BP]

b) In both variants, the pronoun precedes the verb, without a hyphen, in the following cases:

i) After conjunctions (joining words)

enquanto me sinto mal, não quero sair
whilst I feel ill, I don't want to go out

ela fez muito porque se levantou cedo
she has done a lot because she got up early

ii) After adverbs (a few shorter adverbs only, including: **já**, **assim**, **também**, **ainda**)

já te lavaste?
have you got washed yet?

sempre nos sentamos aqui
we always sit here

iii) After "that" clauses (clauses introduced by **que**)

quero que se lembre de mim
I want you to remember me

é uma pena que se tenham levantado tão tarde
it's a shame that they got up so late

iv) In negative sentences

não te lembras?
don't you remember?

ela nunca se lava de manhã
she never has a wash in the morning

v) In interrogatives

como se chama?
what's your name?

onde é que nos sentamos?
where shall we sit?

vi) With **tudo**, **todos**, **ambos**, **toda a gente**

todos me viram
they all saw me

ambas o compraram
they both bought it

c) Position with the gerund

With the gerund (the -ing form of the verb), the object

pronoun follows and is joined by a hyphen, unless there is a negative, or the preposition **em**; with auxiliary verbs such as **estar**, **ir** and **ter**, the pronoun is joined to the auxiliary unless it falls under one of the previous categories of position.

vendo-os...
(on) seeing them...

não a querendo comprar...
not wanting to buy it...

em me vendo, escondia-se
on seeing me, he used to hide

ele foi-o comendo durante o filme
he carried on eating it during the film

não o tendo vendido...
not having sold it...

d) Position with the infinitive

This is a slightly more complex matter, with many more permutations. There follows a brief overview.

i) The direct and indirect object pronoun usually follows the infinitive, joined to it by a hyphen. However, when the infinitive follows a preposition, it is more common for the object pronoun to move in front of the infinitive, although it is often still found after it. The pronouns **o/a/os/as** do not contract and combine with the prepositions **de** and **em** on these occasions.

queria mandá-los
I would like to send them

gostariam de me visitar/gostariam de visitar-me
they would like to visit me

ii) With the preposition **a** (**ao**) and the infinitive, the pronoun goes after the infinitive.

ao comprá-lo, gastou muito
on buying it, he spent a lot of money

iii) With the preposition **por**, if the direct object pronoun is in the third person (**o/a/os/as**), and is not combined with the indirect pronoun (see later sections), then it follows the infinitive.

acabou por dizê-lo a todos
he ended by saying it to everyone

iv) If the infinitive has been made negative, the pronoun goes before it.

para não me ofender
in order not to offend me

e) Position with the past participle

The pronouns do not combine with the past participle in any way. They are linked with the auxiliary verb (the verb used with the past participle) – usually **ter**, **estar**, **ser** and others. Normal rules of position apply.

tinham-no lido
they had read it

não os tenho visitado ultimamente
I haven't visited them recently

f) Position of pronouns with the future and conditional tenses

When a verb in either of the above tenses requires an object pronoun after it, the pronoun is inserted in the following fashion:

main verb part (infinitive) + pronoun + verb ending

eu mandar-te-ei o dinheiro
I shall send you the money

Normal rules of contraction apply:

fá-lo-ia se tivesse tempo
he would do it if he had time

These forms are usually avoided in colloquial language, by omission of the object pronoun, or by uses of other tenses.

mando-te/vou mandar...
faria...

E. CONTRACTED OBJECT PRONOUNS

When a sentence comprises two object pronouns, they join together, or form a contraction with the indirect pronoun first, followed by the direct. The usual rules of position still apply.

Indirect + Direct Sing.	Indirect + Direct Plural
me + **o** > **mo**	**nos** + **o** > **no-lo**
me + **a** > **ma**	**nos** + **a** > **no-la**
me + **os** > **mos**	**nos** + **os** > **no-los**
me + **as** > **mas**	**nos** + **as** > **no-las**
te + **o** > **to**	**vos** + **o** > **vo-lo**
te + **a** > **ta**	**vos** + **a** > **vo-la**
te + **os** > **tos**	**vos** + **os** > **vo-los**
te + **as** > **tas**	**vos** + **as** > **vo-las**
lhe + **o** > **lho**	**lhes** + **o** > **lho**
lhe + **a** > **lha**	**lhes** + **a** > **lha**
lhe + **os** > **lhos**	**lhes** + **os** > **lhos**
lhe + **as** > **lhas**	**lhes** + **as** > **lhas**

dá-mo
give it to me

emprestei-tos
I lent them to you

não mas deu
you didn't give them to me

mandaram-lhas
they sent them to them

Confusion may arise from the type of restricted construction found in this last example. To avoid this kind of ambiguity, use the prepositional forms **a ele**, **a ela**, **aos senhores**, etc.

mandaram-lhas aos senhores
they gave them to you (polite)

mandaram-lhas a eles
they gave them to them (masculine)

Avoidance of contracted forms

These awkward constructions are often spontaneously omitted from Portuguese, particularly in Brazil, as too are the more simple object forms.

empresta-me uma caneta?
can you lend me a pen?

sim, empresto
yes I will (lend it to you)

gostas de vinho tinto?
do you like red wine?

não, não gosto
no, I don't (like it)

F. OBJECT PRONOUNS WITH PREPOSITIONS

a) When object pronouns follow a preposition, they take another form.

Singular		Plural	
mim	me	**nós**	us
ti	you	**vós**	you
ele	him	**eles**	them
ela	her	**elas**	them
si	himself, herself itself, yourself	**si**	themselves, yourselves
você	you, yourself	**vocês**	you, yourselves

ele mora perto de ti
he lives near you

estão todos contra mim
they're all against me

a prenda é para ela
the present is for her

fez o jantar só para si
he made dinner just for himself

começaram sem nós
they started without us

falou sobre vocês
he spoke about you

b) To add clarity to a sentence, the appropriate forms of **mesmo/a/os/as** or **próprio/a/os/as** may be added, both meaning 'self/selves'.

eu trabalho para mim mesma
I work for myself

comprámos o bolo para nós próprios
we bought the cake for ourselves

c) Object pronouns with the preposition **com**

The object pronouns combine with the preposition **com** (with) in the following ways:

Singular	Plural
comigo with me	**connosco** with us **[BP conosco]**
contigo with you	**convosco** with you
com ele with him	**com eles** with them
com ela with her	**com elas** with them
com você with you	**com vocês** with you
consigo with him(self), her(self), your(self)	**consigo** with them(selves) your(selves)

vens connosco?
are you coming with us?

ele precisava de falar comigo
he needed to talk with me

subo consigo
I'll go up with you

Overview of personal pronouns

Subject	Object Direct	Indirect	Reflexive	+ Preposit.	+ com
eu	**me**	**me**	**me**	**mim**	**comigo**
tu	**te**	**te**	**te**	**ti**	**contigo**
ele	**o**	**lhe**	**se**	**ele**	**com ele**
ela	**a**	**lhe**	**se**	**ela**	**com ela**
você *	**o/a**	**lhe**	**se**	**si/você**	**consigo/ com você**
nós	**nos**	**nos**	**nos**	**nós**	**connosco [BP conosco]**
vós	**vos**	**vos**	**vos**	**vós**	**convosco**
eles	**os**	**lhes**	**se**	**eles**	**com eles**
elas	**as**	**lhes**	**se**	**elas**	**com elas**
vocês **	**os/as (vos)**	**lhes (vos)**	**se**	**vocês**	**com vocês (convosco)**

* Also for **o senhor/a senhora**
** Also for **os senhores/as senhoras**

G. DEMONSTRATIVE ADJECTIVES AND PRONOUNS

a) Demonstrative adjectives are used to point out or indicate something or someone. As adjectives, they agree with the noun in number and gender, but unlike other adjectives, demonstratives precede the noun.

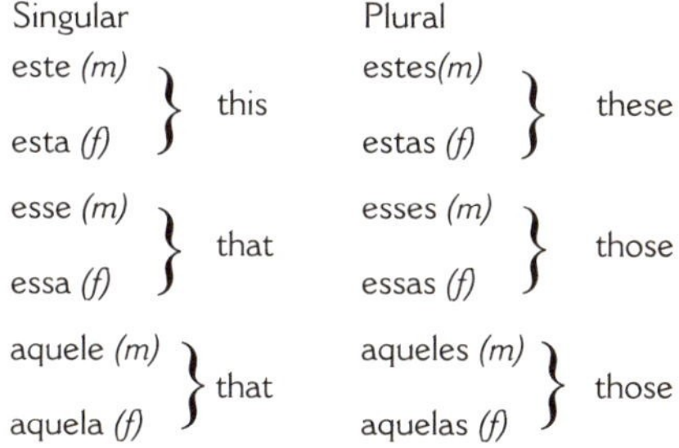

Singular		Plural	
este *(m)* esta *(f)*	this	estes*(m)* estas *(f)*	these
esse *(m)* essa *(f)*	that	esses *(m)* essas *(f)*	those
aquele *(m)* aquela *(f)*	that	aqueles *(m)* aquelas *(f)*	those

There are two ways of expressing "that": **esse** (**essa** etc), used to refer to objects near to the person being addressed, and **aquele** (**aquela** etc), for objects at a distance from both parties.

este hotel
this hotel

essa caneta
that pen (near you)

aquele quadro
that picture

estes sapatos são baratos
these shoes are cheap

aquelas pessoas ali são estrangeiras
those people (over) there are foreigners

b) Demonstrative pronouns

These are identical in form to the demonstrative adjectives above. Additionally, there is a singular, neuter pronoun, which is used to refer to abstract concepts and indefinable objects. The demonstrative pronouns take the place of nouns, and often are translated as "this one" or "that one."

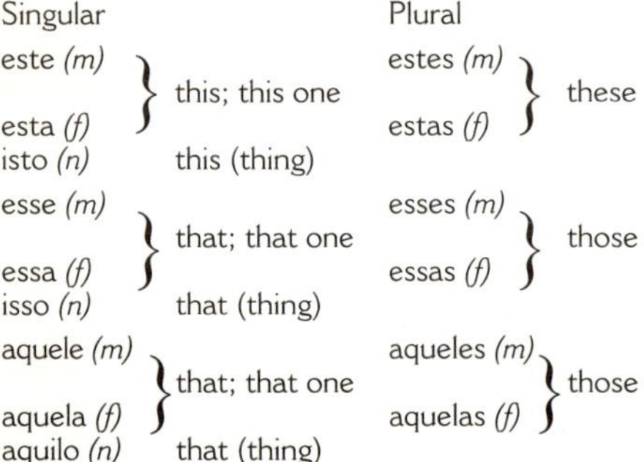

Singular		Plural	
este *(m)*, esta *(f)*	this; this one	estes *(m)*, estas *(f)*	these
isto *(n)*	this (thing)		
esse *(m)*, essa *(f)*	that; that one	esses *(m)*, essas *(f)*	those
isso *(n)*	that (thing)		
aquele *(m)*, aquela *(f)*	that; that one	aqueles *(m)*, aquelas *(f)*	those
aquilo *(n)*	that (thing)		

c) The three neuter demonstratives are invariable – they never change their endings, even when referring to something in the plural.

o que é aquilo? aquilo são batatas
what's that? that, those are potatoes

This means that the invariable demonstratives can be used with both **é** (is) and **são** (are), the verb depending on the item/s.

d) The placing adverbs **aqui** (here), **aí** (there, near the person being addressed), and **ali** (there, away from both parties) are often used with demonstratives.

esta igreja e aquela ali são muito antigas
this church and that one over there are very old

de quem é este bolo?
whose cake is this?

este é da Ana
this one is Ana's

o que é isto?
what is this?

o que é isso que tens aí?
what's that (thing) you've got there?

e) The appropriate forms of **este** and **aquele** can be used to denote "the former" (**aquele**) and "the latter" (**este**).

Manchester e Londres são cidades na Inglaterra; esta fica no sul, aquela no norte
Manchester and London are cities in England; the latter is in the south, the former in the north

a Maria e a Ana são primas; esta mora em Braga e aquela no Porto
Maria and Ana are cousins; the latter lives in Braga and the former in Porto

H. RELATIVE PRONOUNS

a) Relative pronouns and adjectives are used to join, or relate, a dependent clause to the main clause of a sentence. A dependent clause refers to something or someone previously mentioned (the 'antecedent'). The relative pronoun can be the subject or object of a verb, or be preceded by a preposition. The relative pronouns most commonly used are:

que	who, whom, which, that
quem	who, whom
o/a qual (os/as quais)	who, whom, which, that
o que	which

b) Pronouns

i) **Que** refers to both people and things, and can be either a subject or an object. Following a preposition it refers only to things.

o senhor que trabalha no banco é inglês
the man who works in the bank is English

o senhor que vimos no banco é muito velho
the man whom we saw in the bank is very old

esta é a mesa que quero comprar
this is the table (that) I want to buy

a loja em que perdi a mala está fechada
the shop in which I lost my bag is closed

ii) **Quem** is used only to refer to people, and follows a preposition.

a senhora de quem te falei, está por ali
the lady I told you about is over there

este é o meu tio para quem fiz o bolo
this is my uncle for whom I made the cake

iii) **Quem** can also be used without an antecedent, referring to no specific person ('someone/no one').

procuro quem possa pintar a casa
I'm looking for someone who can paint the house

não há quem saiba o nome dela?
is there no one who knows her name?

iv) **O qual** can be used in place of **que**, when referring to people, to avoid ambiguity. The definite article agrees in gender and number with the antecedent. Consider the following ambiguous sentence:

estão a falar com a tia do Paulo, que a minha amiga já conhece
they are talking with Paulo's aunt, who my friend already knows

It is unclear whether the friend knew Paulo or the aunt. The use of the feminine **a qual** in the following sentence leaves no doubt that the reference is to the aunt.

estão a falar com a tia do Paulo, a qual a minha amiga já conhece

v) **O/a qual** is also used with prepositions, especially compound prepositions (consisting of more than one word).

esta é a casa à volta da qual há um muro muito grande
this is the house around which is a large wall

este é o lugar no qual escondi os documentos
this is the place in which (where) I hid the documents

vi) **O que** is a neuter relative used when there is no specific noun as an antecedent. It refers to the preceding phrase or idea as a whole.

nunca me dá flores, o que me irrita
he never gives me flowers, which annoys me

bateu à porta, o que me assustou
he knocked at the door, which frightened me

I. RELATIVE ADJECTIVES

a) **Cujo (-s, -a, -as)** "whose", "of whom", "of which", is a relative adjective, and as such agrees in gender and number with the thing possessed and is used in the same way as the pronouns.

esta é a igreja cuja capela não foi terminada
this is the church whose chapel was not finished

quero ver os meus amigos cujos carros são novos
I want to see my friends whose cars are new.

b) **Quanto (-s, -a, as)** "all that" is often used in the place of **todo o/todos os/tudo o que etc.** ("all of which").

deu ao ladrão todo o dinheiro que tinha
he gave the thief all the money he had
deu-lhe quanto dinheiro tinha

gasto tudo o que ganho
I spend all that I earn
gasto quanto ganho

c) **Onde** (where) and its forms **aonde/para onde** (to where) and **de onde/donde** (from where) are also used in relative clauses and sometimes as an alternative to some of the ones listed above.

casou-se na casa onde (em que/na qual) morava
he got married in the house where he used to live

o porto de onde partimos era muito moderno
the port we departed from was very modern

J. POSSESSIVE PRONOUNS AND ADJECTIVES

Both the possessive pronouns and their corresponding adjectives are identical in form, and both agree in number and gender with the thing possessed, not the possessor. They are both preceded by the definite article, although it often tends to be dropped when using the pronoun. Brazilian Portuguese often omits the article with both pronoun and adjective.

a) Possessive Adjectives

	Singular		Plural	
	Masculine	Feminine	Masculine	Feminine
my	**o meu**	**a minha**	**os meus**	**as minhas**
your*	**o teu**	**a tua**	**os teus**	**as tuas**
his/her/ your**	**o seu**	**a sua**	**os seus**	**as suas**
our	**o nosso**	**a nossa**	**os nossos**	**as nossas**
your (pl)***	**o vosso**	**a vossa**	**os vossos**	**as vossas**
their/ your (pl)**	**o seu**	**a sua**	**os seus**	**as suas**

* Familiar "you"
** **você**/polite "you"
*** Restricted form + **vocês** (colloquially)

o meu irmão
my brother

a tua caneta
your pen

as nossas flores
our flowers

os seus amigos
his (her, your, their) friends

o vosso carro
your car

a sua casa
her (his, your, their) house

b) **O(s) seu(s)** and **a(s) sua(s)** can be ambiguous, as they have a variety of meanings. In order to avoid confusion, the following forms are more often used after the noun to mean "his", "her", "their":

dele	of him (his)
dela	of her (her)
deles	of them *(m)* (their)
delas	of them *(f)* (their)

as calças dele
his trousers

o amigo delas
their friend

as malas dela
her bags

c) Possessive adjectives are used less in Portuguese than in English, especially with parts of the body and clothing which belong to the subject of the verb, and when the possession is obvious. Instead, the definite article is used on its own.

cortei a mão
I cut my hand.

põe o casaco
put your coat on

o que tens no saco?
what have you got in your bag?

d) Possessive pronouns

The forms for possessive pronouns are identical to those for the adjectives. The definite article tends to be omitted after forms of the verb "to be", **ser**. The pronouns agree with the thing possessed. These pronouns take the place of nouns, and are equivalent to the English "mine", "yours", "his", "hers", "its", "ours" and "theirs."

o meu está aqui
mine is here

os nossos estão na cozinha
ours are in the kitchen

esse bolo não é teu
that cake isn't yours

de quem é esta cerveja? é minha
whose beer is this? it's mine

e) To avoid ambiguity in the third person forms, the following forms are often used:

o/a/os/as dele	his
o/a/os/as dela	hers
o/a/os/as deles	theirs *(m)*
o/a/os/as delas	theirs *(f)*

a nossa escola é nova, mas a deles é velha
our school is new, but theirs is old

a mãe do Paulo era simpática; a dela não
Paulo's mother was nice; hers was not

as minhas filhas estudam muito; as deles não
my daughters study a lot; theirs don't

7. NEGATIVES, INTERROGATIVES, EXCLAMATIONS

A. NEGATIVES

Não (no, not) always precedes the verb, but can also follow other words. Portuguese also uses double negatives in the following sequence:

não + verb + another negative

Common negatives

a) não no, not

não falo inglês
I don't speak English

não gostas?
don't you like?

b) nada nothing, not anything

não faz nada
he doesn't do anything

nada muda
nothing changes

não comprei nada
I didn't buy anything

c) ninguém nobody, no one, not anyone

não há ninguém em casa
there is no one at home

ninguém atende
no one's answering

não vimos ninguém
we did not see anyone

d) nenhum/nenhuma no, none, not any

não havia nenhuma resposta
there was no reply

nenhum deles apareceu
none of them turned up

não comprou nenhum
she didn't buy any

The plural forms of **nenhuns** and **nenhumas** are hardly ever used.

For emphasis, the negative can be placed after the noun.

não temos roupa nenhuma
we don't have any clothes at all

e) também não not either, neither

ela não fala alemão; o irmão também não
she does not speak German; her brother does not either

não gosto de tripas. E de fígado? Também não
I don't like tripe. And liver? (I don't like that) either

f) nem (sequer) nor, neither

eles não gostam de vinho nem de cerveja
they don't like wine or beer

g) nem... nem neither... nor

ela come nem peixe nem vegetais
she eats neither fish nor vegetables

não gostaram nem do hotel nem da comida
they didn't like the hotel or the food

h) nem sequer not even

nem (sequer) cumprimenta o vizinho
he doesn't even say hello to his neighbour

i) nunca never, not ever; **jamais** never (stronger)

nunca vou ter suficiente
I'm never going to have enough

não gastou nunca o salário
he never spent his salary

jamais se esquece do primeiro amor
you never forget your first love

j) Negative Responses

In responding to a question in a negative way, Portuguese tends to use a double negative; this can be used with both negatives before the verb, or split. Note, too, how the responses often contain a verb, where in English you would not necessarily use one.

gostam do vinho? – não, não gostamos
do you like the wine? – no, we don't (like it)

vais ao cinema? – não vou, não
are you going to the cinema? – no, I'm not (going)

este é o comboio [BP trem] para Lagos? – não, não é/não é, não
is this the train to Lagos? – no, it isn't

B. INTERROGATIVES (QUESTIONS)

To make a question out of a general statement, simply raise the intonation of your voice at the end of the sentence to make it sound like a question.

comprou um carro
she bought a car

comprou um carro?
did she buy a car? (lit. she bought a car?)

Interrogatives (question words), such as who, what, where, etc, are classified as adjectives, pronouns, or adverbs.

a) Adjectives and Pronouns

i) **que.../o que...** (particularly in conversation) what...?/which...?

que horas são?
what time is it?

o que fizeste?
what did you do?

ii) **quê?/o quê?** (when they stand alone as a question)

sabe uma coisa? o quê?
do you know what? what?

iii) **quem?** who?

quem é aquele senhor?
who is that man?

quem quer vir?
who wants to come?

iv) **qual, quais?** what, which one(s)?

qual é o seu número de telefone?
what is your telephone number?

quais preferes?
which ones do you prefer?

v) **quanto/a?** how much?

quanto custa um bilhete?
how much does a ticket cost?

quanto queijo quer?
how much cheese do you want?

vi) **quantos/as?** how many?

quantos anos tem?
how old are you?
(lit. how many years do you have?)

há quantas casas?
how many houses are there?

b) Adverbs

i) **como...?** how? (in what way/what like)

como se chama?
what are you called?

como está?
how are you?

como é a tua irmã?
what is your sister like?

ii) **quando...?** when?

quando é que chegaste?
when did you arrive?

quando vais partir?
when are you leaving?

iii) **onde...?** where?

onde mora?
where do you live?

onde está o meu livro?
where is my book?

iv) **porque...? [BP por que...?]** why?
porquê? [BP por quê?] why? (when it stands alone)

porque não estudas mais? – porquê? porque não gosto
why don't you study more? – why? because I don't like to

c) Interrogatives with Prepositions

Some of these interrogatives may also be used in conjunction with prepositions. Here are some of the more common ones:

i) **a quem?** to whom?
para quem? for whom?
com quem? with whom?
de quem? of whom, whose?

a quem é que deu o livro?
to whom did you give the book?

para quem é o bolo?
for whom is the cake?

com quem é que ficaste?
who did you stay with?

de quem são estes óculos?
whose are these glasses?

ii) **aonde?** where to?
para onde? where to?
de onde, donde? from where?

aonde vais?
where are you going?

para onde foi depois?
where did you go afterwards?

de onde é? sou de Lisboa
where are you from? I'm from Lisbon

iii) **a que?** at what?
em que? in what/which?
de que? of what?

a que horas chega o avião?
at what time does the plane arrive?

em que dia foi?
on what day did you go?

de que é feito?
what is it made of?

Portuguese questions often use **é que** in an extended interrogative form, (like the French est-ce que) to add emphasis.

onde é que deixaste a mala?
where did you leave your suitcase?

porque é que comprou isto?
why have you bought this?

C. EXCLAMATIONS

a) que! what, what a, how!

que sorte!
what luck!

que bem (que) fala!
how well you speak!

que menina bonita!
what a pretty girl!

b) como! what/how!

como! realmente pensas isto?
what! you really think that?

como é difícil viver assim!
how difficult it is to live like this!

c) quanto/a/os/as! how much/many; what a lot!

quanto estuda o meu filho!
what a lot my son studies!

quantas pessoas!
what a lot of people!

d) qual/quais! what, indeed/how great

qual foi o nosso alívio!
how great was our relief!

quais prêmios!
prizes indeed!

qual o quê!
nonsense!

e) quem! if only I.../would that I... (+ synthetic pluperfect)

quem pudera viajar o mundo!
if only I could travel the world!

quem me dera muito dinheiro!
would that I had a lot of money!

8. VERBS

A. REGULAR CONJUGATIONS

Verbs in Portuguese are divided into three main, regular, groups or conjugations; those ending in:

-ar
-er
-ir

In addition, there are a number of irregular verbs, which do not always follow a given pattern for their endings.

B. SIMPLE TENSES

1. The Present Tense is formed:

a) First conjugation (**-ar**) verbs

To form the present tense of first conjugation verbs, add the following endings to the stem of the verb. (The stem is the part of the infinitive minus the **-ar**/**-er**/**-ir**).

falar to speak: Stem = **FAL-**

Singular		Plural	
eu falO	I speak	**nós falAMOS**	we speak
tu falAS	you speak	**vós falAIS**	you speak
ele/ela falA	he/she speaks	**eles/elas falAM**	they speak
você falA	you speak	**vocês falAM**	you speak

b) Second conjugation (**-er**) verbs

comer to eat: Stem = **COM-**

Singular		Plural	
eu comO	I eat	**eós comEMOS**	we eat
tu comES	you eat	**vós comEIS**	you eat
ele/ela comE	he/she eats	**eles/elas comEM**	they eat
você comE	you eat	**vocês comEM**	you eat

c) Third conjugation (***-ir***) verbs

partir to leave: Stem = **PART-**

Singular		Plural	
eu partO	I leave	**nós partIMOS**	we leave
tu partES	you leave	**vós partIS**	you leave
ele/ela partE	he/she leaves	**eles/elas partEM**	they leave
você partE	you leave	**vocês partEM**	you leave

d) Negative form

To form the negative of a verb, place **não** directly before it.

não falo alemão
I do not speak German

o Pedro não fala bem
Pedro does not speak well

e) Interrogative form

To form a simple question, just raise the intonation of your voice at the end of a sentence. Inversion of subject and verb also takes place (the verb is placed before the subject), but not so frequently. The word "do/does" is not translated.

fala espanhol?
do you speak Spanish?

falam vocês ?
do you speak?

f) The Present tense is used:

i) to express present states:

estou bem
I am well

hoje está frio
it's cold today

ii) to express habitual actions or states:

não como carne
I don't eat meat

levanto-me às 7
I get up at 7

iii) to express general or universal facts:

a vida é dura
life is difficult

o tempo voa
time flies

iv) to express the future:

volto já
I'll be right back

falamos amanhã
we'll talk tomorrow

v) to convey the progressive, or continuous, form:

ele estuda português
he is studying Portuguese

vi) in conjunction with **há** to express a perfect tense:

há uma semana que não vejo a Maria
I haven't seen Maria for a week

2. Imperfect Tense

It is formed by adding the following endings to the stem of the verb:

	-**AR** verbs	-**ER** verbs	-**IR** verbs
eu	+ **ava**	+ **ia**	+ **ia**
tu	+ **avas**	+ **ias**	+ **ias**
ele/ela/você	+ **ava**	+ **ia**	+ **ia**
nós	+ **ávamos**	+ **íamos**	+ **íamos**
vós	+ **áveis**	+ **íeis**	+ **íeis**
eles/elas/vocês	+ **avam**	+ **iam**	+ **iam**

The Imperfect tense is used:

i) to express something that was going on in the past:

faziam muito barulho
they were making a lot of noise

ii) to refer to something that continued over a period of time, as opposed to something that happened at a specific point in time:

enquanto dormiam, alguém levou o carro
while they were sleeping, someone took their car

iii) to describe repeated, or habitual, action that used to take place in the past:

quando era pequeno, nadava todos os dias
when he was young, he used to swim every day

Habitual action can also be expressed by the verb **costumar** in the imperfect:

eu costumava viajar muito
I used to travel a lot

iv) to describe or set the background of a narrative:

chovia muito e o vento soprava
it was raining a lot and the wind was blowing

v) in European Portuguese, as a colloquial replacement for the conditional tense:

gostava de comprar um carro
I would like to buy a car

vi) to express 'polite' wishes:

queria um café
I would like a coffee

vii) to express age in the past:

tinha 8 anos quando fui ao Brasil
I was 8 when I went to Brazil

viii) to express time in the past:

eram 5 horas quando chegou
it was 5 o'clock when he arrived

3. The Preterite Tense

It is formed by adding these endings to the stem.

	-AR verbs	**-ER** verbs	**-IR** verbs
eu	+ **ei**	+ **i**	+ **i**
tu	+ **aste**	+ **este**	+ **iste**
ele/ela/você	+ **ou**	+ **eu**	+ **iu**
nós	+ **ámos** [**BP amos**]	+ **emos**	+ **imos**
vós	+ **astes**	+ **estes**	+ **istes**
eles/elas/vocês	+ **aram**	+ **eram**	+ **iram**

The Preterite, or Simple past (Past definite) tense is used:

i) to express an action that has been completed in the past:

ontem fomos ao teatro
yesterday we went to the theatre

o que bebeste?
what did you drink?

ii) to express the English "have done":

ainda não fiz o trabalho
I have still not done the work

viu o Pedro?
have you seen Pedro?

4. The Pluperfect Tense

Take the 3rd person plural of the Preterite of any verb, remove the ending **-ram**, and add the following set of endings:

-ra/-ras/-ra/-ramos/-reis/-ram

The Pluperfect tense is used, as in English:

i) to express something that had happened in the past:

ele crescera no campo
he had grown up in the countryside

ii) to express a past action completed before another past action:

o rei partira antes da chegada do filho
the king had departed before his son's arrival

iii) in some interesting idiomatic phrases, mostly in the 1st person:

tomara eu/tomáramos nós + infinitive = if only I/we could...
quem me/nos dera + infinitive = if only I/we could...
pudera! rather!

The simple pluperfect tense is only used in written Portuguese, and mostly in literary contexts. In everyday speech and writing, the compound pluperfect is used.

5. The Future Tense

The Future is formed by adding the following endings to the infinitive of all verbs:

	ALL verbs
eu	+ **ei**
tu	+ **ás**
ele/ela/você	+ **á**
nós	+ **emos**
vós	+ **eis**
eles/elas/vocês	+ **ão**

The three irregulars are: **dizer** (to say), which becomes **DIR** + endings, **fazer** (to do/make), which becomes **FAR** + endings, and **trazer** (to bring), becoming **TRAR** + endings.

The Future tense is used:

i) to express future matters:

este Inverno iremos ao Brasil
this winter we'll go to Brazil

não farei o trabalho
I won't do the work

ii) to express conjecture:

onde estará neste momento?
where can he be at this moment?

será que ela me telefona?
I wonder if she will phone me?

The future can also be expressed by using the verb **ir** in the present tense:

vou fazer um bolo
I'm going to make a cake

vão comer fora
they are going to eat out

Note that the future is often expressed by the present tense in Portuguese (see above).

6. The Present Conditional Tense

Like the Future, there is just one set of verb endings, added on to the infinitive of any verb, and the three irregulars mentioned under the Future tense.

	ALL verbs
eu	+ **ia**
tu	+ **ias**
ele/ela/você	+ **ia**
nós	+ **íamos**
vós	+ **íeis**
eles/elas/vocês	+ **iam**

The three irregulars are: **dizer** (to say), which becomes **DIR** + endings, **fazer** (to do/make), which becomes **FAR** + endings, and **trazer** (to bring), becoming **TRAR** + endings.

The Present conditional tense is used:

i) to express a wish or desire:

gostaria de visitar o centro
I would like to visit the town centre

In European Portuguese, the conditional is often replaced by the imperfect tense, especially in the spoken language:

o que gostavas de fazer?
what would you like to do?

ii) to refer to what would happen or what someone would do under certain circumstances:

se ganhasse muito dinheiro, compraria um novo carro
if I won a lot of money, I would buy a new car

o que farias numa casa maior?
what would you do in a larger house?

iii) to express probability in the past:

seriam umas cinco horas
it was probably five o'clock

iv) to express conjecture about the past:

seria que ele estava contente?
was he (really) happy?

C. COMPOUND TENSES

1. The Present Perfect

The present perfect is formed with the present tense of the verb **ter** and the past participle of the main verb.

falar – I have spoken, been speaking, etc.

tenho fal*ado*	**temos fal*ado***
tens fal*ado*	**tendes fal*ado***
tem fal*ado*	**têm fal*ado***

The Present Perfect tense is used to express an action started in the past which usually continues into the present or relates to the present. It may convey an action which has been repeated, or continued a number of times.

tenho trabalhado muito ultimamente
I have (worked) been working a lot lately

os preços têm aumentado
the prices have (gone up) been going up

2. The Pluperfect Tense

The pluperfect is formed by using the imperfect tense of the verb **ter** with the past participle of the main verb. You may also come across **haver** used as the auxiliary verb, particularly in the written language, and especially in Brazil.

falar – I had spoken, you had spoken, etc.

tinha falado	**tínhamos falado**
tinhas falado	**tínheis falado**
tinha falado	**tinham falado**

The Pluperfect tense is used, as detailed earlier:

i) to express something that had happened in the past:

a senhora tinha falado com o gerente
the lady had spoken with the manager

ii) to express a past action completed before another past action:

eu já tinha comido quando eles chegaram
I had already eaten when they arrived

In everyday speech and writing, this compound pluperfect is used. The simple pluperfect is often found in literary work.

3. The Future Perfect Tense

This tense is formed with the future tense of the verb **ter** plus the past participle of the main verb.

comer – I will have eaten, you will have eaten, etc.

terei comido	**teremos comido**
terás comido	**tereis comido**
terá comido	**terão comido**

The Future (perfect) tense is used:

i) to indicate that an action in the future will be completed by the time a second action applies:

terei terminado o trabalho antes das seis horas
I will have finished the work before six o'clock

ii) can be used to express a supposition about the present:

terá chegado?
will he have arrived?

4. The Conditional Perfect

This tense is formed with the conditional of the verb **ter**, plus the past participle of the main verb. In the colloquial language in Portugal, the conditional part of **ter** can be replaced with the Imperfect form.

partir – I would have departed, you would have departed, etc.

teria partido	**teríamos partido**
terias partido	**teríeis partido**
teria partido	**teriam partido**

The Conditional (perfect) tense is used to express what would have happened if something else had not interfered:

se tivessem chegado mais cedo, teriam visto o filme
if they had arrived earlier, they would have seen the film

com mais dinheiro teria comprado o bicicleta
with more money I would have bought the bicycle

5. Position of Pronouns with Perfect tenses

In Perfect tenses, pronouns become connected to the auxiliary verb (**ter**), and not the main verb, which is now in the past participle and not 'strong' enough to hold a pronoun. The normal rules of position still apply.

ultimamente tenho-me levantado cedo
recently I have been getting/got up early

o meu irmão não se tem levantado tão cedo
my brother has not got up so early

D. CONTINUOUS TENSES

The Continuous (progressive) tenses are formed by the appropriate tense of the verb **estar** + **a** + the infinitive of the main verb. In Brazil, **estar** is followed by the gerund. In theory, any tense can be formed into a progressive one, although in practice it is used mostly in the present, imperfect and preterite.

a) It is used to express an action that is, was, or will actually be taking place, or an action that is ongoing:

está a chover [EP]/está chovendo [BP]
it's raining

ela estava a tomar banho [EP]/estava tomando banho [BP]
she was having a bath

b) Other ways of expressing progressive actions are to use the following verbs:

continuar, seguir, ficar, ir, andar

ela continua a frequentar a escola
she continues to go to that school

o Paulo seguia esperando até Maio
Paulo carried on waiting until May

ficámos estudando a semana inteira
we kept on studying all week

vai comendo
carry on eating

eu ando a cantar muito
I'm (going around) singing a lot

E. REFLEXIVE VERBS

A reflexive verb is one where the subject and object of the action are the same person or thing, with the subject acting upon itself. To express this, the verb is used with a reflexive pronoun. The dictionary will indicate whether a verb is reflexive or not, by adding the pronoun -**se** ("self") after it.

sentar-se to sit (oneself) down

Present Tense: I sit (myself) down, you sit (yourself) down, etc.

sento-*me*	**sentamo-*nos****
sentas-*te*	**sentais-*vos***
senta-*se*	**sentam-*se***

sentas-te aqui?
are you sitting here?

os alunos sentam-se sem falar
the pupils sit down without talking

lavar-se to wash oneself

Preterite Tense: I washed myself, you washed yourself, etc.

lavei-*me*	**lavámo-*nos****
lavaste-*te*	**lavastes-*vos***
lavou-*se*	**lavaram-*se***

lavou-se depois do trabalho
he got (himself) washed after the work

lavei-me bem
I had a good wash (washed myself well)

* With the reflexive pronoun, the s is dropped from the verb form of the first person plural when the pronoun follows the verb.

1. Position of the Reflexive Pronoun

In Portugal, the normal position for the pronoun is at the end of the verb, joined to it by a hyphen. In Brazil the reflexive pronoun commonly appears before the verb. In both countries, in negative statements, with questions, and in other circumstances detailed on pages 51-2, the pronoun precedes the verb.

levanta-se às oito
he gets (himself) up at 8 o'clock

[BP] eu me chamo Rivaldo
I'm called Rivaldo (I call myself)

eles nunca se sentam aqui
they never sit here

já te lavaste?
have you washed yourself yet?

Although some verbs, like **atrever-se** (to dare), are always used in the reflexive, others serve a dual purpose, depending on whether they are used with the reflexive pronoun or not.

chamar to call	**chamar-se** to be called
cortar to cut	**cortar-se** to cut oneself
deitar to throw down	**deitar-se** to lie down, to go to bed
lavar to wash	**lavar-se** to have a wash
levantar to lift up, to raise	**levantar-se** to get up, to rise
sentir to sense, to suffer	**sentir-se** to feel, to consider oneself

In fact, you will find that many verbs can be made reflexive in this same way.

2. Reciprocity

The reflexive pronoun may also be used when there is an interaction between plural subjects of a verb; the subjects carry out the action on each other.

vemo-nos todos os dias
we see each other every day

Sometimes, ambiguity about the true meaning, reflexive or reciprocal, may emerge, such as in:

felicitaram-*se* = they congratulated themselves OR they congratulated each other

In order to avoid this problem, the following additions may be useful.

um ao outro/uma à outra (to) one another, each other
uns aos outros/umas às outras (to) one another (plural)
mutuamente mutually

felicitaram-se um ao outro
they congratulated each other

F. RADICAL-CHANGING VERBS

A number of verbs in Portuguese change their spelling slightly in the present indicative tense. The change occurs in the stem of the verb in all persons except the **nós** and **vós** forms. As the present subjunctive is based on the first person singular of the present indicative, its correct spelling is a vital starting point for the formation of the subjunctive (see page 101).

Here are some of the more common types of radical changing verbs:

a) First conjugation, **-ar**

boiar to float
bóio, bóias, bóia, boiamos, boiais, bóiam
A written accent is added.

recear to fear
receio, receias, receia, receamos, receais, receiam
An *i* is added.

Verbs ending in **-ear** also following this pattern include: **passear** (to go for a walk/stroll), **cear** (to have supper), **pentear(-se)** (to comb) and **barbear** (to shave).

odiar to hate
odeio, odeias, odeia, odiamos, odiais, odeiam
An *e* is added.

Other similar verbs to **odiar** include: **incendiar** (to set fire to), **negociar** (to negotiate), **ansiar** (to yearn for), **remediar** (to remedy) and **premiar** (to reward).

b) Second conjugation, **-er**

moer to grind
moo, móis, mói, moemos, moeis, moem
Also: **roer** (to nibble), **doer** (to hurt).

c) Third conjugation, **-ir**

The majority of changes occur in these verbs. The changes take place in the first person singular only, and will therefore carry over to the present subjunctive.

i) *e* changes to *i*

conseguir to achieve/manage	**consigo** I manage
despir to undress	**dispo** I undress
divertir to enjoy	**divirto** I enjoy
ferir to wound	**firo** I wound

mentir to lie	**minto** I lie
preferir to prefer	**prefiro** I prefer
repetir to repeat	**repito** I repeat
seguir to follow	**sigo** I follow
sentir to feel	**sinto** I feel
servir to serve	**sirvo** I serve
vestir to dress	**visto** I dress

agredir to assault
agrido, agrides, agride, agredimos, agredis, agridem
The *i* is kept in four parts of the verb.

Also like **agredir**: **denegrir** (to denigrate), **prevenir** (to warn, prevent), **progredir** (to progress), **transgredir** (to transgress).

iii) *o* changes to *u*

cobrir to cover	**cubro** I cover
descobrir to discover	**descubro** I discover
dormir to sleep	**durmo** I sleep
engolir to swallow	**engulo** I swallow

polir to polish becomes: **pulo, pules, pule, polimos, polis, pulem**

iii) *u* changes to *o*

subir to go up
subo, sobes, sobe, subimos, subis, sobem

Here, the change occurs three times.

Also: **acudir** (to run to help), **bulir** (to move/stir), **consumir** (to consume), **cuspir** (to spit), **fugir** (to flee), **sacudir** (to shake), **sumir** (to hide).

iv) *i* changes to *í*

possuir to possess
possuo, possuis, possui, possuímos, possuís, possuem

Also: **instruir** (to instruct), **obstruir** (to obstruct). **Construir** (to construct) and **destruir** (to destroy) follow **possuir** but may also have alternative forms as follows:

destruo, destruis/destróis, destrui/destrói, destruímos, destruís, destruem/destroem

d) Others

A small number of other verbs (which are otherwise considered regular) have an irregularity in the first person singular only, which affects the consequent spelling of the subjunctive form.

medir to measure	**meço** I measure
ouvir to hear	**ouço/oiço** I hear
pedir to ask for	**peço** I ask for
perder to lose	**perco** I lose
poder to be able to	**posso** I can

G. ORTHOGRAPHIC-CHANGING VERBS

Orthographic-changing verbs are those which require a slight modification in their spelling (orthography) in order to maintain the pronunciation of the infinitive. The spelling change takes place on the last consonant of the stem of the verb before certain vowels, as listed below. The most common changes are as follows:

a) Verbs ending in **-car** before an 'e' the *c* changes to *qu*, to maintain a hard 'c'-sound.

ficar to stay **fico** I stay **fiquei** I stayed

Other verbs of this type are:

acercar-se	to approach
brincar	to play
colocar	to place
explicar	to explain
indicar	to indicate
modificar	to modify
multiplicar	to multiply
publicar	to publish
sacar	to remove
tocar	to touch; to play (instrument)

b) Verbs ending in **-çar**

Before *e*, the *ç* changes to *c*, as the cedilla is no longer required to maintain a soft 'c'-sound.

caçar to hunt **caço** I hunt **cacei** I hunted

Other verbs of this type are:

almoçar	to have lunch
ameaçar	to threaten
calçar	to put on shoes
começar	to begin

c) Verbs ending in **-gar**

Before *e*, the *g* becomes *gu* to maintain the hard 'g' sound.

chegar to arrive **chego** I arrive **cheguei** I arrived

Other verbs of this type are:

apagar	to extinguish
entregar	to hand over
jogar	to play
julgar	to judge

obrigar	to compel; to oblige
pagar	to pay
prolongar	to prolong

d) Verbs ending in **-cer**

Before a or o, the c becomes ç to maintain the soft 'c' (s) sound.

conhecer to know **conheço** I know **conhece** he knows

Other verbs of this type include:

acontecer	to happen
agradecer	to thank
aquecer	to heat
descer	to descend
esquecer	to forget
merecer	to deserve
obedecer	to obey
parecer	to seem, to appear
reconhecer	to recognise

e) Verbs ending in **-ger** and **-gir**

Before *a* or *o*, the g becomes *j* to maintain the soft 'g' sound.

fugir to flee **fujo** I flee **foge** he flees

Other verbs of this type are:

abranger	to include, to comprise
afligir	to afflict; to distress
corrigir	to correct
dirigir	to drive; to direct
eleger	to elect
exigir	to demand; to require
fingir	to pretend
proteger	to protect

f) Verbs ending in **-guer** and **-guir**

Before *a* or *o*, gu simply becomes *g* to maintain the hard 'g' sound.

seguir to follow   **sigo** I follow   **segue** he follows

Other verbs of this type are:

conseguir	to achieve; to obtain
distinguir	to distinguish
erguer	to erect
perseguir	to pursue; to persecute

You will also come across examples of far rarer verbs whose orthography changes.

H. IMPERSONAL AND DEFECTIVE VERBS

Impersonal verbs are those which are found mostly in the 3rd person singular or plural. Some are known as 'defective' verbs, as they might not have a full range of tenses. Others may be used with an indirect object pronoun where you would not find one in the English. A selection of the most common follows but they are not particularly widespread.

a) Weather verbs

Some of the common verbs are: **chover** (to rain), **nevar** (to snow), **chuviscar** (to drizzle), **gelar** (to freeze), **trovoar** (to thunder), as well as various expressions using **fazer** and **haver**.

nunca neva aqui
it never snows here

ontem gelou
yesterday it froze

fazia sol todos os dias
it was sunny every day

no norte há vento
it is windy in the north

b) **Anoitecer** (to get dark – nightfall)/**amanhecer** (to get light – dawn)

no Inverno anoitece mais cedo
in winter it gets dark earlier

o dia amanheceu com sol
the day dawned with sun

c) Verbs taking pronouns

To translate "to appeal to/to fancy doing...", the verb **apetecer** is used with the indirect object pronoun.

apetece-te sair? – não, não me apetece
do you fancy going out? – no, I don't (fancy that)

Parecer, the verb "to appear" or "to seem", can be used in a similar way to convey a colloquial expression of "to think" – in the sense of "it seems to me..."

que lhes parece?
what do you think?

parecia-nos estranho
it seemed strange to us

Interessar (to interest) can be used in exactly the same way – so you can say "something gives interest to me".

interessam-me as línguas
languages interest me

não lhe interessa nada
he is not interested in anything

d) Faltar, fazer falta, sobrar

Faltar translates "to be missing, lacking", and with an indirect pronoun, means "to be short of".

faltavam 20 euros
there were 20 euros missing/short

falta ar aqui
there's a lack of air here

falta-nos uma peça
we are short of a piece

Fazer falta can mean "to be necessary", and with a pronoun, "to need/miss"

um dicionário fazia falta
a dictionary was needed

não me faz falta o tempo inglês
I do not miss the English weather

Sobrar means "to be more than enough" and "to have left over":

sobrava comida
there was food left over

sobraram-me 20 euros
I had 20 euros left over

e) Doer – when something hurts

To talk about a part of the body hurting in Portuguese, you use **doer** in the singular (if only one part hurts) or the plural (if more than one bit is sore). The indirect object pronoun is also used.

dói-me a perna
my leg hurts

doem-lhe os olhos
her eyes hurt

onde te dói?
where does it hurt you?

f) Haver

Haver (to have) appears mainly in the 3rd person, translating "there is/are" in the present tense, but also used in many other tenses.

há um turismo por aqui?
is there a Tourist Office round here?

havia muitas pessoas na rua
there were many people in the street

se houver paz no mundo...
if there is peace in the world...

g) Miscellaneous

Acontecer – to happen

o que aconteceu?
what has happened?

acontece assim...
it happens like this...

Custar – to cost

um selo custa 2 euros
a stamp costs 2 euros

quanto custaram os bolos?
how much did the cakes cost?

Tratar-se de – to be about

o livro trata-se duma aventura
the book is about an adventure

de que se tratava o filme?
what was the film about?

Jazer – to lie (be laid down) – used for graves

aqui jaz/jazem...
here lies/lie...

Soer – to usually happen

tais cosas soem acontecer nas férias
such things usually happen in the holidays

I. THE SUBJUNCTIVE

The subjunctive mood is another set of verbal structures used in various tenses, for such circumstances as the giving of commands; the expression of desire, hope and influence; after certain conjunctions or expressions; and in general, whenever situations described appear to be doubtful, hazy or uncertain.

Tenses of the Subjunctive

1. Present
2. Imperfect
3. Future
4. Present Perfect
5. Pluperfect (Past Perfect)
6. Future Perfect

1. Formation

a) Present Subjunctive

With the exception of the irregular verbs **dar**, **estar**, **ser**, **ir**, **haver**, **saber** and **querer**, all other verbs, including any which may change their spelling, form the present subjunctive in the same way. The stem is that of the first person singular of the present indicative, and the following endings are added:

	-AR verbs	**-ER** verbs	**-IR** verbs
eu	+ **e**	+ **a**	+ **a**
tu	+ **es**	+ **as**	+ **as**
ele/ela/você	+ **e**	+ **a**	+ **a**
nós	+ **emos**	+ **amos**	+ **amos**
vós	+ **eis**	+ **ais**	+ **ais**
eles/elas/vocês	+ **em**	+ **am**	+ **am**

FALAR	**COMER**	**PARTIR**
1st person = **falo**	1st person = **como**	1st person = **parto**
fale	**coma**	**parta**
fales	**comas**	**partas**
fale	**coma**	**parta**
falemos	**comamos**	**partamos**
faleis	**comais**	**partais**
falem	**comam**	**partam**

pedir First person singular: **peço**

peça

peças

peça

peçamos

peçais

peçam

This illustrates the importance of using the stem of the first person singular, instead of relying on that of the infinitive.

For the subjunctive tenses of a number of verbs, including common irregular verbs, see the verb tables on pages 151-67.

espero que amanhã faça sol
I hope it's sunny tomorrow

lamento que não possas vir à festa
I'm sorry that you can't come to the party

quer que ajudemos?
do you want us to help?

b) Imperfect Subjunctive

The imperfect subjunctive is formed by adding the following endings onto the stem of the third person plural of the preterite (indicative). Again, following this rule is particularly important where irregular verbs are concerned.

	-AR verbs	**-ER** verbs	**-IR** verbs
eu	+ **asse**	+ **esse**	+ **isse**
tu	+ **asses**	+ **esses**	+ **isses**
ele/ela/você	+ **asse**	+ **esse**	+ **isse**
nós	+ **ássemos**	+ **êssemos**	+ **íssemos**
vós	+ **ásseis**	+ **êsseis**	+ **ísseis**
eles/elas/vocês	+ **assem**	+ **essem**	+ **issem**

FALAR 3rd pers. Pret = **FALARAM**	**COMER** 3rd pers. Pret = **COMERAM**	**PARTIR** 3rd pers. Pret = **PARTIRAM**
falasse	**comesse**	**partisse**
falasses	**comesses**	**partisses**
falasse	**comesse**	**partisse**
falássemos	**comêssemos**	**partíssemos**
falásseis	**comêsseis**	**partísseis**
falassem	**comessem**	**partissem**

Like the present subjunctive, there are a number of uses for the imperfect tense, which will be dealt with more fully later.

oxalá ganhasse na loteria!
if only he could win the lottery!

era preferível que não trabalhasses tanto
it would be better if you didn't work so much

se eu fosse você...
if I were you...

c) Future Subjunctive

The future subjunctive is also based on the stem of the third person plural of the preterite indicative, onto which are added the following endings:

	-AR verbs	**-ER** verbs	**-IR** verbs
eu	+ **ar**	+ **er**	+ **ir**
tu	+ **ares**	+ **eres**	+ **ires**
ele/ela/você	+ **ar**	+ **er**	+ **ir**
nós	+ **armos**	+ **ermos**	+ **irmos**
vós	+ **ardes**	+ **erdes**	+ **irdes**
eles/elas/vocês	+ **arem**	+ **erem**	+ **irem**

FALAR 3rd pers. Pret = **FALARAM**	COMER 3rd pers. Pret = **COMERAM**	PARTIR 3rd pers. Pret = **PARTIRAM**
falar	**comer**	**partir**
falares	**comeres**	**partires**
falar	**comer**	**partir**
falarmos	**comermos**	**partirmos**
falardes	**comerdes**	**partirdes**
falarem	**comerem**	**partirem**

fazer: Third person Preterite: **fizeram**; Stem: **FIZ**; Future Subj.: fizer

The future subjunctive is used when referring to indefinite or hypothetical future situations. In this context, it often follows such conjunctions as **quando** ("when"), **assim que** ("as soon as"), **se** ("if"), **logo que** ("as soon as"), **conforme** ("depending on whether") and **enquanto** ("while"), among others.

assim que chegarmos, vamos para a praia
as soon as we arrive, let's go to the beach

se fores lá, compra um jornal
if you go there, buy a paper

quando o tempo estiver melhor, vou andar de bicicleta
when the weather's better, I'm going out on my bicycle

d) Present Perfect Subjunctive

For all verbs this is formed with the present subjunctive of the verb **ter**, plus the past participle of the main verb.

comprar First person singular of **ter**: **tenho**;

Subjunctive: **tenha**

tenha comprado
tenhas comprado
tenha comprado
tenhamos comprado
tenhais comprado
tenham comprado

talvez eles já tenham chegado
perhaps they have already arrived

espero que tenhas comido tudo
I hope that you have eaten everything

duvido que ela tenha terminado
I doubt that she's finished

e) Pluperfect (Past Perfect) Subjunctive

For all verbs this is formed with the imperfect subjunctive of the verb **ter**, plus the past participle of the main verb.

beber Third person plural of **ter**: **tiveram**; Imperfect Subj.: **tivesse**

tivesse bebido
tivesses bebido
tivesse bebido
tivéssemos bebido
tivésseis bebido
tivessem bebido

se tivesse estado bem, ela tinha ido ao teatro
if she had been well, she would have gone to the theatre

quem me dera que tivesse estudado mais
if only I had studied more

embora tivessem visitado o monumento, não gostaram muito
although they had visited the monument, they didn't like it much

f) Future Perfect Subjunctive

For all verbs this is formed by the future subjunctive of **ter**, plus the past participle of the main verb.

abrir Third person plural of **ter**: **tiveram**; Future Subj.: **tiver**

tiver aberto
tiveres aberto
tiver aberto
tivermos aberto
tiverdes aberto
tiverem aberto

quando tiveres terminado os estudos, o que queres fazer?
when you have finished your studies, what do you want to do?

assim que tiver feito o bolo, podes provar
as soon as I've made the cake, you can try it

se o dinheiro não tiver chegado até à sexta-feira, telefone-me
if the money hasn't arrived by Friday, phone me

2. Expressing emotion, doubt, desire, influence

The subjunctive is used after verbs that fall into this category. The verb in the subordinate clause, – that part of the sentence that generally follows the word **que**, ("that") – is in the subjunctive, *ie* the subjunctive is not in the verb introducing the emotion, but in the one resulting in that emotion, wish etc.

a) Verbs commonly used to express influence (desire/wish/orders) include:

aconselhar	to advise
não admitir	to not allow
consentir	to consent to
desejar	to want, to desire
dizer	to say, to tell
esperar	to hope, to wish
implorar	to implore, to beg
mandar	to order
negar	to deny
pedir	to ask for
permitir	to allow/permit
persuadir	to persuade
precisar	to need
preferir	to prefer
proibir	to forbid
querer	to wish/want

não admito que me trate assim
I won't allow you to treat me this way

ele disse ao mendigo que se fosse embora
he told the beggar to go away

queriam que pintasse a casa de amarelo
they wanted him to paint the house yellow

Note: if the desire expressed relates to oneself, the infinitive construction is used.

espero que visite Coimbra
I hope you visit Coimbra

espero visitar Coimbra
I hope to visit Coimbra

b) Verbs Expressing Emotion

All types of emotions expressed towards another party, such as anger, happiness, sadness, fear, place the verb following **que** in the subjunctive as above. Typical verbs of emotion include:

alegrar-se	to be glad
estranhar	to be surprised
lamentar	to be sorry
recear	to fear/worry
sentir	to feel; to feel sorry
temer	to fear
ter medo	to be frightened
ter pena de	to be sorry (for)
ter pena que	to be sorry (that)

alegro-me que possas vir
I'm happy that you can come

sentia muito que ela estivesse doente
he was sorry that she was ill

estranhámos que eles tivessem gasto tudo
we were surprised that they had spent everything

c) Verbs Expressing Doubt

ter dúvidas que	to have doubts that
duvidar	to doubt

tenho dúvidas que ela saiba tanto
I doubt that she knows so much

duvidamos que chegues à hora certa
we doubt that you'll arrive on time

3. Impersonal Expressions and Verbs of Opinion

a) The subjunctive is used after expressions which are

termed 'impersonal'; in English, these expressions usually begin with "it." The expressions may be in any tense, although in practice you will find them mostly in the Present (with references to actions generally in the future), and Imperfect (for actions in the past). Here is a selection of the more common expressions – they all take the word **que** (that) after them, and it is the verb following **que** that goes into the subjunctive:

basta que	it is enough that
é bom que	it is good
convém que	it is convenient/appropriate that
é conveniente	it is convenient
é estranho que	it is strange
é importante que	it is important
é incrível que	it is incredible
é lógico que	it is logical
é melhor que	it is better/best
é natual que	it is natural
é necessário que	it is necessary
é possível que	it is possible that
é preciso que	it is necessary
é provável que	it is probable that
é suficiente que	it is sufficient/enough

é provável que fiquemos em casa
it is probable that we'll stay at home (we'll probably stay at home)

era lógico que estudasse muito
it was logical that he studied a lot

será necessário que traga os documentos
it will be necessary for you to bring your documents (you'll need to ...)

b) When the following expressions indicate true or clear-cut situations, the verbs are in the indicative mood. However, when they are used in the negative, as contrary to fact, the following verb goes into the subjunctive again.

é certo	it is true; it is certain
é evidente	it is evident
é manifesto	it is clear
é óbvio	it is obvious
é verdade	it is true

é óbvio que eles gostam da comida
it is obvious that they like the food

não é óbvio que eles gostem da comida
it is not obvious that they like the food

é verdade que tenho muitos amigos
it is true that I have a lot of friends

não é verdade que eu tenha um gato
it is not true that I have a cat

c) Impersonal expressions can, of course, also be used with the infinitive, if the dependent verb has no definite subject.

é importante pagar as contas
it is important to pay the bills

era possível levar crianças
it was possible to take children

d) Verbs of Opinion

The verbs of thinking and believing take the indicative mood when in the affirmative, but in the negative assume the subjunctive after them.

achar que	to think/reckon that
crer que	to believe that
julgar que	to think/judge that
parecer que	to seem (to one) that
pensar que	to think that

acho que vale a pena ler este livro
I think it is worth reading this book

não acho que valha a pena ler este livro
I don't think it is worth...

parecia-nos que ela estava feliz
it seemed to us that she was happy
(she seemed happy to us)

não nos parecia que ela estivesse feliz
it didn't seem to us that she was happy
(she didn't seem happy to us)

e) Special Expressions

These special expressions employ both the present and future subjunctives – the present in the first verb, and the future in the second one:

seja o que for whatever it may be
seja como for however it may be
seja quanto for however much it may be
seja quando for whenever it may be
esteja onde estiver wherever I, he, she, you or it may be
venha o que vier come what may
custe o que custar at whatever cost

This construction can be applied to many other verbs.

It can also be used to describe past circumstances and events, with both verbs in the imperfect subjunctive.

fosse o que fosse
whatever it might be

estivesse onde estivesse
wherever he, she, you or it might be

4. Subjunctive: Conjunctions and Hypothesis

a) There are a variety of conjunctions and expressions of hypothesis (assumption) that are followed by a verb in the subjunctive, in any tense. A selection of the most used follows below:

a fim de que	in order that
ainda quando	even if
ainda que	although
ainda se	even if
a não ser que	unless
antes que	before
até que	until
conquanto	although
contanto que	provided that
desde que	as long as/provided that
embora	although
logo que	as soon as
mesmo que	even if
nem que	(not) even if
(no) caso (que)	in (the) case (that)
para que	in order that
posto que	although
primeiro que	before
se bem que	although
sem que	without
sob condição que	on condition that

tens que te esforçar mais, a fim de que ganhes boas notas
you have to try harder in order to get good results

embora estivesse doente, foi à discoteca
although she was ill, she went to the disco

não faço isto, nem que me pague
I won't do this, even if you pay me

mesmo que chova, vamos ao parque
even if it's raining, we're going to the park

sem que vejas o carro, não podes dizer se vais gostar ou não
if you don't see the car, you won't be able to say whether you like it or not

logo que possamos, compramos os bilhetes
as soon as we can, we'll buy the tickets

b) talvez and **oxalá**

The subjunctive is used after the adverb **talvez** ("perhaps, maybe") and the interjection **oxalá**, from the Arabic ("god [Allah] willing; hopefully"). Some people also still use the expression: **Deus queira que** (God willing = hopefully).

talvez ela venha amanhã
perhaps she will come tomorrow

oxalá não chova
let's hope is doesn't rain

Deus queira que tudo corra bem consigo
let's hope everything turns out well for you (God willing, everything will...)

c) Special Expressions

The following expressions also call for the subjunctive:

como quer que however
(por/para...) onde quer que wherever
por mais que however much
por muito(s) que however much (many)
por pouco que however little
quando quer que whenever
(a/de...) quem quer que whoever

para onde quer que vá, leva sempre muito dinheiro
wherever he goes to, he always takes a lot of money

por mais que tente, nunca consigo emagrecer
however much I try, I never manage to slim

quem quer que apareça, há comida para todos
whoever appears, there is food for everyone

5. Subjunctive: Indefinite and Negative Antecedents

In relative clauses introduced by **que**, the subjunctive is used when the antecedent (the person or thing immediately preceding **que**) is not definite or specific. This may be in terms of the article, for example ("the" is definite, "a" is not), or when the antecedent refers to "someone" or "anyone". A negative antecedent, such as "nobody", also calls for the subjunctive.

quero comprar um carro que não seja demasiado velho
I want to buy a car that isn't too old

andamos à procura de alguém que saiba consertar botas
we are looking for someone who knows how to repair boots

não há ninguém aqui que possa ajudar
there is no one here who can help

Compare:

vamos a uma praia que fique muito longe
we're going to a beach that's a long way off

vamos à praia que fica muito longe
we're going to the beach that's a long way off

J. "IF" CLAUSES

Clauses containing the word "if" are known as conditional clauses, because the word **se** (if) imposes some condition upon the action. The clauses may state an action which is very likely, or certain to happen, possibly on a regular basis, in which case the verb in the clause remains in the indicative mood. The subjunctive is used in sentences containing a clause stating an action which is doubtful to happen, or contrary to fact. The subjunctive is also used after **se** when referring to future actions.

a) Open possibility – present tense

The verb in the "if" clause goes into the present indicative, the main clause may be present, future or an imperative (command).

se gosto de qualquer coisa, pois compro
if I like something then I buy it

se não gostas da matemática, nunca vais ser engenheiro!
if you don't like maths, you'll never be an engineer!

se estão a cantarolar, pois que parem!
if you are humming, then stop it!

b) Facts about the past – past tense

When simply stating facts about events which took place in the past, **se** can be used with the indicative past tenses.

se fazia sol, íamos à piscina todos os dias
if it was sunny, we used to go (we went) to the swimming pool every day

c) **se** = whether

When **se** means "whether", it is followed by the indicative tenses. It is used in this sense most often with the verb **saber** – to know.

não sei se posso ir contigo
I don't know (if) whether I can go with you

não sabia se jogava ou não
he did not know (if) whether he was playing or not

d) Hypothetical, doubtful actions, contrary to fact – Imperfect Subjunctive

When expressing "conditions", *ie* actions subject to doubt, imaginary situations, and actions which may or may not have a solution, the **se** clause uses the imperfect subjunctive. The verb in the main clause can go in the conditional (indicative) tense or, in colloquial (European) Portuguese, the conditional (indicative) can be replaced by the imperfect tense.

se eu fosse você, iria (ia) ao médico
if I were you, I would go to the doctor's

se tivesse mais tempo, faria (fazia) um bolo
if I had more time I would make a cake

se não falassem tanto, aprenderiam (aprendiam) muito mais
if they didn't talk so much, they would learn so much more

e) Actions contrary to the statement – past conditionals

When a statement declares something contrary to what actually happened (or did not happen) in the past, use the pluperfect subjunctive in the "if" clause, and the main verbs in the imperfect indicative, conditional, or compound tenses of the two.

se não tivessem comprado tanto, poderiam (podiam) ter ido ao cinema
if they hadn't bought so much, they could have gone to the cinema

se não tivesse perdido o bilhete, já seria (era) milionária
if you had not lost the ticket, you would now be a millionaire

se tivesse estudado mais, poderia (podia) ter sido professor
if I had studied more, I could have been a teacher

f) **se** and the future

Se is used with the future subjunctive when referring to an action in the future.

The verbs in the main part of the sentence can go in the present or future indicative, or imperative.

se eu for ao centro, compro-te uns selos
if I go to town, I'll buy (lit. I buy) you some stamps

se não houver tempo, ficaremos só 10 minutos
if there is not enough time, we'll just stay 10 minutes

se falar com ela, diga que passo lá amanhã
if you speak to her, tell her that I'll pass by tomorrow

g) **se**...? = what if...?

You can start a question with **se**..., or **e se**..., when you want to express "what if...?". The verb in the **se** clause goes into the subjunctive in the relevant tense. This construction is widely used in spoken Portuguese.

e se o João vier mais tarde?
(and) what if João comes later?

se eles não tivessem conseguido entrar?
what if they hadn't been able to get in?

h) Como se... = as if/though...

Use the imperfect or pluperfect subjunctive in this type of construction.

era como se não visse nada
it was as if she couldn't see anything

é como se não tivessem feito nada
it's as if/though they hadn't done anything

K. THE IMPERATIVE – COMMANDS

Commands are the way you tell people to do, or not to do things. You can 'command' a single person, or many people. The verb of the action you wish to happen or not happen will change its endings according to whether you are commanding someone in the **tu** form, the old **vós** form, or the **você** and **vocês** forms (and their polite equivalents).

a) Affirmative Commands

i) The **tu** Form

The command form for **tu** (used with friends, family, young children, and people of similar social rank) is exactly the same verb form as the third person singular of the present indicative.

abrir to open	**abre** (3rd person)	**abre!** Open!
comer to eat	**come** (3rd person)	**come!** Eat!
falar to speak	**fala** (3rd person singular)	**fala!** Speak!

fala mais devagar!
speak more slowly!

come as cenouras!
eat the carrots!

abre-me esta lata!
open this can for me!

The same system applies to irregular verbs: take the 3rd person singular of the present tense.

IR – vai por aqui go along here
FAZER – faz o trabalho do the work
VIR – vem cá come here
[* SER = **sê** in the **tu** form**]**

ii) The **vós** Form

The archaic **vós** form is still used in church services, political speeches, and by older people in remote areas. The command form for **vós** is also based on the present indicative. The final 's' is simply removed from the second person plural (**vós**) form of the verb.

cantar to sing	**cantais** (2nd person pl)	**cantai!** Sing!
receber to receive	**recebeis** (2nd person)	**recebei!** Receive!
resistir to resist	**resistis** (2nd person)	**resisti!** Resist!
ir to go	**ides** (2nd person)	**ide!** Go!

trabalhai companheiros!
work (my) comrades

resisti às tentações do mundo
resist the temptations of the world

vinde pastores...
come shepherds (first line of *O come all ye faithful*)

iii) The **você** Form, or Polite command

To command in the **você** (or 3rd person polite) form (used with strangers, older people, and those of higher social rank; used exclusively in most of Brazil), the verb goes into the present subjunctive. There are one or two irregulars – check the verb tables on pages

151-67 for common irregular verbs, and watch out for spelling changes in the first person.

comprar to buy	**compra** (3rd person)	**compre!** buy!
dizer to say	**digo** (1st person)	**diga!** say!
escrever to write	**escreve** (3rd person)	**escreve!** write!
estar to be		**esteja!** be!
insistir to insist	**insiste** (3rd person)	**insiste!** insist!

compre um jornal
buy a newspaper

beba tudo
drink it all

suba as escadas
go up the steps

tenha a bondade...
be so kind...

iv) The **vocês** Form, or Plural command

As above, the **vocês** form goes into the subjunctive, in the 3rd person plural. Its formation is as described above.

abrir to open	**abrem** (3rd person)	**abram!** open!
beber to drink	**bebem** (3rd person)	**bebam!** drink!
lavar to wash	**lavam** (3rd person plural)	**lavem!** wash!
saber to know		**saibam!** know!
seguir to follow	**sigo** (1st person)	**sigam!** follow!

andem mais rápido
walk more quickly

escrevam em inglês
write in English

decidam vocês
you decide

façam menos barulho
make less noise

b) Negative Commands

All commands in the negative use the appropriate subjunctive form. Don't forget to move the position of any reflexive pronouns if you are using a reflexive verb, or any other object pronouns which may be involved.

abrir to open — **não abra (você)** don't open!
correr to run — **não corrais (vós)** do not run!
esperar to wait — **não esperes (tu)** don't wait!
ter to have — **não tenha (o senhor)** don't have!
trazer to bring — **não tragam (vocês)** don't bring!

não te cortes
don't cut yourself

não respondais
don't respond

não admita nada
don't admit anything

não me digam mentiras
don't tell me lies

c) Polite Commands

i) Requests can be softened by using the construction **fazer favor** + **de** + infinitive.

faz favor de fechares a janela
please close the window

faça favor de escolher
please choose

façam favor de me emprestar uma caneta
please lend me a pen

ii) The same type of polite request can be made by using **querer** (to want, wish) + infinitive, or **ter a bondade de** (to have the kindness to) + infinitive.

quer abrir a janela para mim?
would you mind opening the window for me?

queres ajudar?
would you help?

queira abrir a mala?
would you open the case?

tenham a bondade de levar este saco
would you be so kind as to take this bag?

iii) Infinitives can also be used to convey instructions to the masses, especially on public notices.

não fumar!
no smoking!

pagar ao motorista
pay the driver

não abrir
don't open

iv) In everyday Portuguese, it is also very common to 'tell' someone to do something by 'asking' them by using the present tense, especially with people you know.

fazes-me isto?
will you do this for me? (do this for me will you)

compras cigarros, sim?
buy some cigarettes, will you?

v) **Que** can be used with the subjunctive to soften a command, or for emphasis.

que tenhas boa sorte!
may you have good luck!

que estejam todos felizes
may they all be happy

que fale primeiro o José
let José speak first

d) i) To encourage, or exhort, in the first person plural (we form), as "let's...", the present subjunctive is used:

atravessemos!
let's cross!

ii) This is more commonly replaced by **vamos** + the infinitive

vamos cantar
let's sing

L. THE INFINITIVE

The infinitive of a verb in Portuguese is the form that corresponds in English to "to do", *eg* **falar** = to speak. It is the form of the verb you will find in a dictionary, before you manipulate its endings to say who is carrying out the action and when. In Portuguese, verbs fall into one of three verb groups, known as "conjugations": those ending in:

1) -ar (the most common) *eg* **falar** to speak

2) -er *eg* **comer** to eat

3) -ir *eg* **partir** to leave

There are also a number of irregular verbs which do not belong to these groups, and have peculiarities in their formation.

a) The General Infinitive

Infinitives appear in the following situations:

i) After other verb forms, as they might in English

quero ver o filme
I want to see the film

não podemos ir
we are not able to go (we cannot go)

ela deve estudar mais
she ought to (must) study more

têm que comprar leite
they have to buy milk

ii) After prepositions and verbs taking a preposition. See also pages 145-6.

antes de sair, jantei
before going out, I had dinner

gosto de ver futebol
I like to watch (watching) football

esqueceu-se de mandar um cartão
he forgot to send a card

iii) Impersonally, in expressions such as:

nadar é uma boa actividade
swimming is a good activity

não é fácil fazer isto
it isn't easy to do this

iv) As an impersonal command form, often on signs in public places:

não pisar a relva!
don't walk on the grass

pagar à caixa!
pay at the check-out

v) As a noun, with the definite article **o**:

o fumar faz mal
smoking is bad for you

o beber leite faz bem
drinking milk is good for you

b) The Personal Infinitive

This type of infinitive is personalized – it can be used in its inflected forms (with endings) to refer to whoever is performing the action. It is formed by adding the endings listed below onto the infinitive of any verb.

eu (I) – no ending	**nós** (we) + **-mos**
tu (you) + **-es**	**vós** (you) + **-des**
ele (he) – no ending	**eles** (they) + **-em**
ela (she) – no ending	**elas** (they) + **-em**
você etc (you) – no ending	**vocês etc** (you plural) + **-em**

falar to speak	**dizer** to say	**partir** to leave
falar	**dizer**	**partir**
fala*res*	**dize*res***	**parti*res***
falar	**dizer**	**partir**
falar*mos*	**dizer*mos***	**partir*mos***
falar*des*	**dizer*des***	**partir*des***
falar*em*	**dizer*em***	**partir*em***

Usage

In many cases, the personal infinitive can provide a much simpler alternative to complex constructions, such as those requiring the subjunctive form of the verb, and is therefore a valuable linguistic tool. The following are its uses:

a) With impersonal expressions:

não seria melhor tu partires já?
wouldn't it be better if you left now?

é incrível eles estarem cá
it is incredible that they are here

The meaning of the last example is identical to that of the subjunctive construction:

é incrível que eles estejam *or* **estivessem cá**

b) After prepositions:

ao termos tentado, conseguimos abrir a porta
having tried, we managed to open the door

não quis continuar sem eles aparecerem
he did not want to continue without them appearing

c) After prepositional phrases:

These phrases, amongst others, may be followed by the personal infinitive: **antes de** ("before"), **depois de** ("after"), **no caso de** ("in case; if"), **apesar de** ("in spite of").

antes de te ires embora, escreve o teu novo endereço
before you go away, write down your new address

depois de termos visitado cinco vezes, conhecemos bem o lugar
after we had visited five times, we knew the place well

no caso delas chegarem cedo, vou já preparar o jantar
in case they arrive early, I'm going to get dinner ready now

apesar de vocês jogarem bem, não vão participar no concurso
in spite of your playing well, you are not going to take part in the competition

d) Distinguishing between verb subjects

The personal infinitive is often used in a sentence describing two separate actions, where there are different subjects for each verb.

ao chegarem as cartas, ela leu-as uma por uma
when the letters arrived, she read them one by one

depois de tu teres partido, o teu primo chegou
after you had set off, your cousin arrived

However, it can also be used when the subjects are the same:

depois de jantarmos, fomos ao teatro
after dining, we went to the theatre

apesar de ter chegado imediatamente, não pude encontrar o cão
despite having arrived quickly, I could not find the dog

no caso de te sentires mal, diz-me logo
if you feel ill, tell me straight away

e) Commands

The personal infinitive is also used with **é favor** as a formal imperative, especially in business contexts (written or spoken), and in public announcements.

é favor enviarem pagamento dentro dum prazo de 30 dias
please send payment within 30 days

é favor os senhores passageiros não fumarem dentro da carruagem
will passengers please refrain from smoking inside the carriage.

M. PARTICIPLES

Participles are parts of verbs, sometimes used on their own, but often in conjunction with other verbs; there is a present and a past participle.

a) Present participle

This conveys the form of the verb which corresponds in English to '-ing'. It is also known as the gerund.

It is formed as follows: add these endings to the stem of any verb:

-AR verbs	-ER verbs	-IR verbs
+ **ando**	+ **endo**	+ **indo**

pôr = **pondo**

These endings are the same for whichever person is doing the action.

falando speaking **comendo** eating
partindo departing

The gerund is used:

i) To substitute a (second or third) main verb in a sentence which is a follow-on action from a previous verb – instead of having a list of completed actions, one of them may become a gerund.

subiram a rua escutando música e dançando
they went up the street listening to music and dancing

ii) To substitute time expressions such as **quando** (when) + main verb, or **ao** (on) + infinitive.

chegando ao trabalho, fiz um café
arriving at work (when I arrived at work), I made a coffee

vendo o amigo, foi ter com ele
on seeing his friend, he went over to him

iii) To indicate how something is happening – as a response to the question **como**?

saiu da casa correndo
she ran out of the house

como é que partiu a perna? esquiando
how did he break his leg? skiing

iv) Brazilians use the gerund form in continuous tenses, where in Portugal the construction **estar** + **a** + infinitive is used.

ela estava dormindo quando chegaram
she was sleeping when they arrived

que está fazendo?
what are you doing?

b) ir + Gerund

The verb **ir** (to go) is used with the gerund to express a situation where someone is 'getting on with' or 'carrying on with' an action.

vão praticando, que eu já vou
you carry on practising, I'll be there soon

enquanto o Pedro foi ao médico, a Ana foi limpando a casa
whilst Pedro went to the doctor's, Ana carried on tidying the house

vai preparando o almoço, que eu volto à meio-dia
you get on with preparing lunch, as I'll be back at mid-day

c) Past Participle

The past participle of a verb is what corresponds (in regular verbs) to the English "-ed", *eg* To finish > finished, To walk > walked, To paint > painted. Past participles in Portuguese are used in compound tenses – those made up of two verbs (**ter** + the action verb), such as "have painted", or "will have walked". They are also used extensively acting as adjectives, with the verbs to be (**ser** and **estar**), and along with **ficar** (to stay, remain, become), **andar** (to walk, frequent, act in a certain way – colloquially), **ir** (to go) and **vir** (to come). They also form part of the Passive Voice (see next section).

The past participle for regular verbs is formed as follows: add these endings to the stem of any verb:

-AR verbs	-ER verbs	-IR verbs
+ **ado**	+ **ido**	+ **ido**

The endings are the same for any person. However, when the participles are used as adjectives, their endings change according to the normal rules of agreement.

eu tinha pintado a parede
I had painted the wall

ela não tem respondido às chamadas
she has not been responding to calls

nós teremos chegado no sábado
we will have arrived on Saturday

a porta está fechada
the door is closed

a janela foi partida
the window was broken

d) Irregular Verbs – Irregular Past Participles

Some irregular verbs come with an irregular past participle. Here are the main ones – you can also refer to the verb tables on pages 151-67.

dizer to say	**dito** said
fazer to do/make	**feito** done/made
pôr to put	**posto** put
ver to see	**visto** seen
vir to come	**vindo** come (same as the gerund)

e) Double Participles

There are also a number of verbs in Portuguese that have two past participles. The regular one, formed as explained above, is used in the compound tenses, and does not change its ending, but the irregular forms are the ones used with the verbs **ser** and **estar**, **ficar**, **andar**, **ir** and **vir**, and will change their endings as adjectives. Following are some verbs which act in this way. Where only one form is given, that form must be used exclusively.

		Regular (used in tenses)	Irregular (with **ser/estar etc**)
abrir	to open	-	**aberto**
aceitar	to accept	**aceitado**	**aceite**
acender	to light	**acendido**	**aceso**
completar	to complete	**completado**	**completo**
eleger	to elect	**elegido**	**eleito**

entregar	to hand over	**entregado**	**entregue**
enxugar	to dry	**enxugado**	**enxuto**
escrever	to write	-	**escrito**
expulsar	to expel	**expulsado**	**expulso**
fritar	to fry	**fritado**	**frito**
ganhar	to win	-	**ganho**
gastar	to spend	-	**gasto**
limpar	to clean	**limpado**	**limpo**
matar	to kill	**matado**	**morto**
omitir	to omit	**omitido**	**omisso**
pagar	to pay	-	**pago**
prender	to fasten/ arrest	**prendido**	**preso**
romper	to tear	**rompido**	**roto**
salvar	to save	**salvado**	**salvo**
secar	to dry	**secado**	**seco**
soltar	to let loose	**soltado**	**solto**
suspender	to suspend	**suspendido**	**suspenso**

o ladrão ficou preso
the thief was arrested

a sessão foi suspensa
the session was suspended

tinham limpado o quarto
they had cleaned their room

não lhes tenho escrito
I have not been writing to them

a conta foi paga
the bill was paid

a toalha está seca
the towel is dry (dried)

N. THE PASSIVE

An ordinary sentence is made up of a subject, a verb, an object, and whatever adjectives, adverbs or other types of words are necessary to give any further appropriate information. A sentence with the word order Subject-Verb-Object is said to be in the active voice. In the active voice, the subject performs the action of the verb. However, the word order can be changed without altering the meaning of the sentence. If the subject then receives the action of the verb, or is acted upon by the object, the sentence is said to belong to the passive voice.

a) In Portuguese, the passive voice is formed with **ser**, in any tense, and the past participle of the verb. The past participle agrees with the subject of the verb in number (singular or plural) and gender (masculine or feminine). The person or thing carrying out the action, known as "the agent", is introduced by **por** ("by") and its combinations. It is not always necessary to show the agent.

Compare:

o João pintou a casa a casa foi pintada pelo João
João painted the house the house was painted by João

b) The passive is particularly useful when the agent is not known:

durante as férias a casa foi pintada
during the holidays the house was painted

c) A range of tenses can be represented:

o professor não é respeitado pelos alunos
the teacher is not respected by the pupils

este livro foi escrito por Saramago
this book was written by Saramago

os carros vão ser lavados pelos escoteiros
the cars are going to be washed by the scouts

todas as blusas tinham sido vendidas pela empregada
all the blouses had been sold by the shop assistant

The agent can be omitted if it is unknown or indefinite.

o país foi invadido
the country was invaded

a loja tinha sido atacada
the shop had been attacked

d) **estar** + Past Participle

Estar may be used with a past participle to describe a state resulting from an action. Again, the past participle agrees in number and gender, just as an adjective would, and can be used with any tense.

a farmácia está fechada
the pharmacy is closed

a porta estava aberta
the door was open

e) Remember that some verbs have two sets of past participles: one to be used with the auxiliary verb **ter**, the other for use with **ser** and **estar** (see previous section).

f) Reflexive Substitute for the Passive

Often, the reflexive pronoun **se** is used to convey the passive form, particularly when the subject of the verb is unknown, undetermined, or irrelevant to comprehension of the phrase. It is seen on many public signs and notices. **Se** is placed next to the verb according to the normal rules of positioning. The verb is in the active voice in the third person, either singular or plural, depending on the context.

aqui fala-se inglês
English is spoken here

alugam-se apartamentos
apartments to rent

não se ouviram as notícias
the news was not heard

Often the same meaning can be conveyed by simply using the third person plural:

um preço foi combinado
a price was agreed

combinaram um preço
they agreed a price

g) Impersonal Use of **se**

Se can be used with the third person singular to express an indefinite subject ("it," "they," "one", "you".) This is a similar concept to the French use of "on" (one).

como se diz isto em português?
how do you say this in Portuguese?

como se escreve o seu nome?
how do you write your name?

como é que se vai para...?
how do you get to...?

O. MODAL AUXILIARY VERBS – MUST/OUGHT/SHOULD/COULD

The verbs **dever**, **ter de/que**, **precisar de** and **haver de** are all used to convey "having to do something". To translate situations involving the word "could" = "be able", the verb **poder** is used. Different tenses can be used for a variety of situations. The verbs are known here as 'auxiliaries' because they are all used in combination with a main verb in the infinitive.

a) dever

Can convey moral obligation – what you must, must not, should or should not do – and is often used in giving advice to people. It also expresses probability, in ideas of supposition.

um jogador de futebol deve comer bem
a football player must eat well

não deveriam comer gorduras
they shouldn't (ought not to) eat fat

onde está a minha mãe? Deve ter ido ao mercado
where is my mother? She must have gone to the market

deverias ter comprado um jornal
you should have (ought to have) bought a newspaper

b) ter de/que (interchangeable)

Conveys a strong necessity to carry out an action – what you "have to" do, often when there is obligation from outside forces. It is used very much in everyday Portuguese.

tenho de comprar fósforos
I have to buy matches

tens que estudar mais
you have to study more

tem que te relaxar
you have to relax

tínhamos de reservar lugares
we had to reserve places

c) precisar de

Conveys general need, or necessity.

preciso de ver o médico
I need to see the doctor

vamos precisar de mais 20 euros
we're going to need 20 more euros

precisava de sair da casa
he needed to get out of the house

d) haver de

Conveys a strong intention or conviction in respect of future action or situations. It can translate into English in a variety of ways, such as: "really have to", "got to", "really will", "will", where emphasis stresses the fact or idea expressed.

havemos de ganhar qualquer dia
we've got to win some day

ele há-de [BP há de] ser piloto
one day he will be a pilot

hei-de [BP hei de] aprender esta língua
I WILL learn this language

e) poder

Conveys possibility and opportunity to do things, in the negative says what you are not allowed to do, and is also used to ask and give permission. It translates in different tenses as "can" and "could". Its basic meaning is "to be able to", and is followed by verbs in the infinitive.

não pode trabalhar mais
he cannot work any more

posso entrar? Pode, sim
can I come in? Yes, you can

poderiam ter comprado mais
they could have bought more

não podias ouvir bem?
could you not hear well?

P. IRREGULAR VERBS

Irregular verbs are those that do not follow the normal pattern for endings in some, or all, tenses. This section illustrates a dozen of the most commonly-used irregular verbs, across the present, preterite, and imperfect tenses, with examples. For a more comprehensive coverage, refer to the verb tables on pages 151-67.

a) Present

dar to give	**dizer** to say	**estar** to be	**fazer** to do/ make
dou	**digo**	**estou**	**faço**
dás	**dizes**	**estás**	**fazes**
dá	**diz**	**está**	**faz**
damos	**dizemos**	**estamos**	**fazemos**
dais	**dizeis**	**estais**	**fazeis**
dão	**dizem**	**estão**	**fazem**

haver to have	**ir** to go	**poder** to be able	**pôr** to put
hei	**vou**	**posso**	**ponho**
hás	**vais**	**podes**	**pões**
há	**vai**	**pode**	**põe**
havemos	**vamos**	**podemos**	**pomos**
haveis	**ides**	**podeis**	**pondes**
hão	**vão**	**podem**	**põem**

ser to be	**ter** to have	**ver** to see	**vir** to come
sou	**tenho**	**vejo**	**venho**
és	**tens**	**vês**	**vens**
é	**tem**	**vê**	**vem**
somos	**temos**	**vemos**	**vimos**
sois	**tendes**	**vedes**	**vindes**
são	**têm**	**vêem**	**vêm**

nunca dou dinheiro aos mendigos
I never give money to beggars

sempre dizes a verdade?
do you always tell the truth?

onde está a Maria?
where is Maria?

fazemos bons bolos
we make good cakes

há um banco na esquina
there is a bank on the corner

ides para a igreja?
are you going to church?

não podem nadar hoje
they cannot swim today

ponho a mesa às seis
I set the table at 6

és a minha melhor amiga
you are my best friend

tem um quarto?
do you have a room?

vemos a televisão todos os dias
we watch TV every day

eles vêm também?
are they coming too?

b) Preterite

dar to give	**dizer** to say	**estar** to be	**fazer** to do/ make
dei	**disse**	**estive**	**fiz**
deste	**disseste**	**estiveste**	**fizeste**
deu	**disse**	**esteve**	**fez**
demos	**dissemos**	**estivemos**	**fizemos**
destes	**dissestes**	**estivestes**	**fizestes**
deram	**disseram**	**estiveram**	**fizeram**

haver to have	**ir** to go	**poder** to be able	**pôr** to put
houve	**fui**	**pude**	**pus**
houveste	**foste**	**pudeste**	**puseste**
houve	**foi**	**pôde**	**pôs**
houvemos	**fomos**	**pudemos**	**pusemos**
houvestes	**fostes**	**pudestes**	**pusestes**
houveram	**foram**	**puderam**	**puseram**

ser to be	**ter** to have	**ver** to see	**vir** to come
fui	**tive**	**vi**	**vim**
foste	**tiveste**	**viste**	**vieste**
foi	**teve**	**viu**	**veio**
fomos	**tivemos**	**vimos**	**viemos**
fostes	**tivestes**	**vistes**	**viestes**
foram	**tiveram**	**viram**	**vieram**

dei o meu livro ao Pedro
I gave my book to Pedror

o que disseste?
what did you say?

a Ana esteve cá
Ana has been/was here

não fizemos nada
we haven't done anything/we did nothing

houve muitas pessoas lá
there were many people there

fui ao mercado
I went to the market

pudeste entrar?
where you able to get in?

onde pôs o saco?
where did you put the bag?

o filme foi bom
the film was good

tivemos muita sorte
we were very lucky

quem viu o acidente?
who saw the accident?

vieram de táxi
they came by taxi

c) Imperfect

dar to give	**dizer** to say	**estar** to be	**fazer** to do/ make
dava	**dizia**	**estava**	**fazia**
davas	**dizias**	**estavas**	**fazias**
dava	**dizia**	**estava**	**fazia**

dávamos	**dizíamos**	**estávamos**	**fazíamos**
dáveis	**dizíeis**	**estáveis**	**fazíeis**
davam	**diziam**	**estavam**	**faziam**

haver to have	**ir** to go	**poder** to be able	**pôr** to put
havia	**ia**	**podia**	**punha**
havias	**ias**	**podias**	**punhas**
havia	**ia**	**podia**	**punha**
havíamos	**íamos**	**podíamos**	**púnhamos**
havíeis	**íeis**	**podíeis**	**púnheis**
haviam	**iam**	**podiam**	**ppunham**

ser to be	**ter** to have	**ver** to see	**vir** to come
era	**tinha**	**via**	**vinha**
eras	**tinhas**	**vias**	**vinhas**
era	**tinha**	**via**	**vinha**
éramos	**tínhamos**	**víamos**	**vínhamos**
éreis	**tínheis**	**víeis**	**vínheis**
eram	**tinham**	**viam**	**vinham**

dava tudo para morar aqui
I would give everything to live here

dizia-me as horas, por favor?
would (could) you tell me the time, please?

estávamos numa floresta
we were in a forest

sempre fazia o trabalho cedo
she always did her work early

havia uma igreja aqui, mas já não há
there used to be a church here, but it's not here anymore

iam comprar uma casa
they were going to buy a house

podias ter viajado com ela
you could have travelled with her

nunca punha casaco para sair
I never used to put a coat on to go out

eram sete horas
it was 7 o'clock

tinha um gato chamado Fofo
I used to have a cat called Fluffy

viam uma raposa durante a noite
they used to see a fox at night

o gato vinha ao meu emprego
the cat used to come to my work

Q. VERBS FOLLOWED BY A PREPOSITION

Some verbs require a preposition after them when used before an infinitive. The equivalent English verbs may not always require a preposition, and, when they do, the preposition may not necessarily correspond with the one in Portuguese.

a) Verbs + **a**

acostumar-se a	to get used to
ajudar a	to help to
animar a	to encourage to
aprender a	to learn how to
atrever-se a	to dare to

autorizar a	to authorize to
começar a	to begin to
compelir a	to compel to
convidar a	to invite to
decidir-se a	to decide to
ensinar a	to teach how to
forçar a	to force to
habituar a	to accustom to
incitar a	to incite to
levar a	to cause to
meter-se a	to set out to
obrigar a	to oblige to
ocupar-se a	to busy oneself with
pôr-se a	to start
resignar-se a	to resign oneself to

nunca me acostumei a viver aqui
I've never got used to living here

decidiram-se a pintar a casa
they decided to paint the house

ele vai ocupar-se a pintar a casa
he's going to be busy painting the house

b) Verbs + **de**

acabar de	to finish ...ing
acusar de	to accuse of
alegrar-se de	to be glad to
arrepender-se de	to repent
cansar-se de	to get tired of
cessar de	to cease ...ing

contentar-se de	to content oneself with
deixar de	to stop
desculpar de	to forgive for
desesperar de	to despair of
dissuadir de	to dissuade from
encarregar-se de	to undertake
envergonhar-se de	to be ashamed of
esquecer-se de	to forget to
fartar-se de	to get tired of
gostar de	to like
impedir de	to prevent from
lembrar-se de	to remember to
parar de	to stop
precisar de	to need to

acabou de cortar a relva
he finished cutting the lawn

cansaram-se de estudar
they got tired of studying

não te desculpo de ter perdido o meu livro
I can't forgive you for having lost my book

esqueceste-te da minha festa?
did you forget my party?

não me lembrei de comprar leite
I didn't remember to buy milk

precisamos de sair mais
we need to go out more

c) Verbs + **em**

comprazer-se em	to take pleasure in
concordar em	to agree to
consentir em	to consent to
consistir em	to consist of
convir em	to agree to
empenhar-se em	to insist on ...ing
fazer bem em	to do well to
fazer mal em	to do wrong to
hesitar em	to hesitate to
insistir em	to insist on
pensar em	to think of
perserverar em	to persevere in
persistir em	to persist in
teimar em	to insist on
vacilar em	to hesitate to

ela compraz-se em cozinhar
she takes pleasure in cooking

não convim em comprar a casa
I did not agree to buy the house

hesitaram em aceitar os resultados
they hesitated to accept the results

vamos persistir em estudar esta língua
let's persist in studying this language

d) Verbs + **por**

acabar por	to end up
começar por	to begin by
esforçar-se por	to make an effort

estar por	to be yet to be done
lutar por	to fight to
pelejar por	to fight to
principiar por	to begin by
suspirar por	to long to
terminar por	to end by
trabalhar por	to work to

acabou por viajar pelo mundo
she ended up travelling the world

lutaram por lá ficar
they fought to stay there

termino por vos dizer...
I finish by saying to you...

e) Verbs + **com**

conformar-se com	to resign oneself to
contar com	to count on
sonhar com	to dream of

Verbs + **para**

estar para	to be about to
preparar-se para	to prepare to
servir para	to serve to

conto com chegar cedo
I'm counting on arriving early

sonhava com visitar o Brasil
she dreamed of visiting Brazil

conformou-se com vender o carro
he resigned himself to selling the car

está para partir
it is about to depart

prepararam-se para lutar
they prepared to fight

isto serve para cortar plástico
this serves to cut (is for cutting) plastic

f) Some of these verbs are also used with their preposition when followed by a noun. In these cases, when the articles (definite and indefinite) are present, you must remember to combine them with the preposition, according to the rules of contraction, *eg* **do**, **das**, **dumas** *etc*.

ela resignou-se ao trabalho
she resigned herself to the work

lembrou-se das laranjas
he remembered the oranges

nunca vamos concordar nisto
we're never going to agree on this

temos de lutar pelos direitos
we have to fight for our rights

sonho com dias de sol
I dream of sunny days

preparava-se para o baile
she was getting ready for the dance

A. CONJUGATION TABLES

The following verbs provide the main patterns of conjugation, including the conjugation of some common irregular verbs. They are arranged in alphabetical order.

-ar verb	**ANDAR**
-er verb	**COMER**

-ir verb	**PARTIR**
Reflexive verb	**SENTAR-SE**
Auxiliary verb	**TER**
Modal auxiliary verbs	**DEVER** **HAVER** **PODER**
Common irregular verbs	**DAR** **DIZER** **ESTAR** **FAZER** **IR** **PÔR** **SER** **VER** **VIR**

'Harrap Portuguese Verbs', a fully comprehensive list of Portuguese verbs and their conjugations is also available in this series.

ANDAR to walk; to ride (bicycle, etc)

PRESENT	IMPERFECT	FUTURE
1. ando	andava	andarei
2. andas	andavas	andarás
3. anda	andava	andará
1. andamos	andávamos	andaremos
2. andais	andáveis	andareis
3. andam	andavam	andarão

PRETERITE	PERFECT	PLUPERFECT
1. andei	tenho andado	andara
2. andaste	tens andado	andaras
3. andou	tem andado	andara
1. andámos	temos andado	andáramos
2. andastes	tendes andado	andáreis
3. andaram	têm andado	andaram

PLUPERFECT (Compound)
tinha andado etc

FUTURE PERFECT
terei andado etc

CONDITIONAL

PRESENT	PERFECT	*IMPERATIVE*
1. andaria	teria andado	
2. andarias	terias andado	anda
3. andaria	teria andado	ande
1. andaríamos	teríamos andado	andemos
2. andaríeis	teríeis andado	andai
3. andariam	teriam andado	andem

SUBJUNCTIVE

PRESENT	IMPERFECT	FUTURE
1. ande	andasse	andar
2. andes	andasses	andares
3. ande	andasse	andar
1. andemos	andássemos	andarmos
2. andeis	andásseis	andardes
3. andem	andassem	andarem

PERFECT	PLUPERFECT	FUTURE PERFECT
tenha andado etc	tivesse andado etc	tiver andado etc

INFINITIVE	*PERSONAL INFINITIVE*		*PARTICIPLE*
PRESENT andar	1. andar	1. andarmos	**PRESENT** andando
PAST ter andado	2. andares	2. andardes	**PAST** andado
	3. andar	3. andarem	

COMER to eat

	PRESENT	IMPERFECT	FUTURE
1.	como	comia	comerei
2.	comes	comias	comerás
3.	come	comia	comerá
1.	comemos	comíamos	comeremos
2.	comeis	comíeis	comereis
3.	comem	comiam	comerão

	PRETERITE	PERFECT	PLUPERFECT
1.	comi	tenho comido	comera
2.	comeste	tens comido	comeras
3.	comeu	tem comido	comera
1.	comemos	temos comido	comêramos
2.	comestes	tendes comido	comêreis
3.	comeram	têm comido	comeram

PLUPERFECT (Compound)
tinha comido etc

FUTURE PERFECT
terei comido etc

CONDITIONAL

	PRESENT	PERFECT
1.	comeria	teria comido
2.	comerias	terias comido
3.	comeria	teria comido
1.	comeríamos	teríamos comido
2.	comeríeis	teríeis comido
3.	comeriam	teriam comido

IMPERATIVE

come
coma
comamos
comei
comam

SUBJUNCTIVE

	PRESENT	IMPERFECT	FUTURE
1.	coma	comesse	comer
2.	comas	comesses	comeres
3.	coma	comesse	comer
1.	comamos	comêssemos	comermos
2.	comais	comêsseis	comerdes
3.	comam	comessem	comerem

PERFECT	PLUPERFECT	FUTURE PERFECT
tenha comido etc	tivesse comido etc	tiver comido etc

INFINITIVE

PRESENT comer
PAST ter comido

PERSONAL INFINITIVE

1. comer	1. comermos
2. comeres	2. comerdes
3. comer	3. comerem

PARTICIPLE

PRESENT comendo
PAST comido

DAR to give

PRESENT	IMPERFECT	FUTURE
1. dou	dava	darei
2. dás	davas	darás
3. dá	dava	dará
1. damos	dávamos	daremos
2. dais	dáveis	dareis
3. dão	davam	darão

PRETERITE	PERFECT	PLUPERFECT
1. dei	tenho dado	dera
2. deste	tens dado	deras
3. deu	tem dado	dera
1. demos	temos dado	déramos
2. destes	tendes dado	déreis
3. deram	têm dado	deram

PLUPERFECT (Compound)
tinha dado etc

FUTURE PERFECT
terei dado etc

CONDITIONAL

PRESENT	PERFECT	*IMPERATIVE*
1. daria	teria dado	
2. darias	terias dado	dá
3. daria	teria dado	dê
1. daríamos	teríamos dado	dêmos
2. daríeis	teríeis dado	dai
3. dariam	teriam dado	dêem

SUBJUNCTIVE

PRESENT	IMPERFECT	FUTURE
1. dê	desse	der
2. dês	desses	deres
3. dê	desse	der
1. dêmos	déssemos	dermos
2. deis	désseis	derdes
3. dêem	dessem	derem

PERFECT	PLUPERFECT	FUTURE PERFECT
tenha dado etc	tivesse dado etc	tiver dado etc

INFINITIVE

PRESENT dar
PAST ter dado

PERSONAL INFINITIVE

1. dar	1. darmos
2. dares	2. dardes
3. dar	3. darem

PARTICIPLE

PRESENT dando
PAST dado

DEVER to have to; to owe

PRESENT	IMPERFECT	FUTURE
1. devo	devia	deverei
2. deves	devias	deverás
3. deve	devia	deverá
1. devemos	devíamos	deveremos
2. deveis	devíeis	devereis
3. devem	deviam	deverão

PRETERITE	PERFECT	PLUPERFECT
1. devi	tenho devido	devera
2. deveste	tens devido	deveras
3. deveu	tem devido	devera
1. devemos	temos devido	devêramos
2. devestes	tendes devido	devêreis
3. deveram	têm devido	deveram

PLUPERFECT (Compound)
tinha devido etc

FUTURE PERFECT
terei devido etc

CONDITIONAL

PRESENT	PERFECT	*IMPERATIVE*
1. deveria	teria devido	
2. deverias	terias devido	deve
3. deveria	teria devido	deva
1. deveríamos	teríamos devido	devamos
2. deveríeis	teríeis devido	devei
3. deveriam	teriam devido	devam

SUBJUNCTIVE

PRESENT	IMPERFECT	FUTURE
1. deva	devesse	dever
2. devas	devesses	deveres
3. deva	devesse	dever
1. devamos	devêssemos	devermos
2. devais	devêsseis	deverdes
3. devam	devessem	deverem

PERFECT	PLUPERFECT	FUTURE PERFECT
tenha devido etc	tivesse devido etc	tiver devido etc

INFINITIVE
PRESENT dever
PAST ter devido

PERSONAL INFINITIVE
1. dever
2. deveres
3. dever
1. devermos
2. deverdes
3. deverem

PARTICIPLE
PRESENT devendo
PAST devido

DIZER to say, to tell

PRESENT	IMPERFECT	FUTURE
1. digo	dizia	direi
2. dizes	dizias	dirás
3. diz	dizia	dirá
1. dizemos	dizíamos	diremos
2. dizeis	dizíeis	direis
3. dizem	diziam	dirão

PRETERITE	PERFECT	PLUPERFECT
1. disse	tenho dito	dissera
2. disseste	tens dito	disseras
3. disse	tem dito	dissera
1. dissemos	temos dito	disséramos
2. dissestes	tendes dito	disséreis
3. disseram	têm dito	disseram

PLUPERFECT (Compound)
tinha dito etc

FUTURE PERFECT
terei dito etc

CONDITIONAL

PRESENT	PERFECT	*IMPERATIVE*
1. diria	teria dito	
2. dirias	terias dito	diz(e)
3. diria	teria dito	diga
1. diríamos	teríamos dito	digamos
2. diríeis	teríeis dito	dizei
3. diriam	teriam dito	digam

SUBJUNCTIVE

PRESENT	IMPERFECT	FUTURE
1. diga	dissesse	disser
2. digas	dissesses	disseres
3. diga	dissesse	disser
1. digamos	disséssemos	dissermos
2. digais	dissésseis	disserdes
3. digam	dissessem	disserem

PERFECT	PLUPERFECT	FUTURE PERFECT
tenha dito etc	tivesse dito etc	tiver dito etc

INFINITIVE
PRESENT dizer
PAST ter dito

PERSONAL INFINITIVE
1. dizer — 1. dizermos
2. dizeres — 2. dizerdes
3. dizer — 3. dizerem

PARTICIPLE
PRESENT dizendo
PAST dito

ESTAR to be

PRESENT	IMPERFECT	FUTURE
1. estou	estava	estarei
2. estás	estavas	estarás
3. está	estava	estará
1. estamos	estávamos	estaremos
2. estais	estáveis	estareis
3. estão	estavam	estarão

PRETERITE	PERFECT	PLUPERFECT
1. estive	tenho estado	estivera
2. estiveste	tens estado	estiveras
3. esteve	tem estado	estivera
1. estivemos	temos estado	estivéramos
2. estivestes	tendes estado	estivéreis
3. estiveram	têm estado	estiveram

PLUPERFECT (Compound)
tinha estado etc

FUTURE PERFECT
terei estado etc

CONDITIONAL

PRESENT	PERFECT	*IMPERATIVE*
1. estaria	teria estado	
2. estarias	terias estado	está
3. estaria	teria estado	esteja
1. estaríamos	teríamos estado	estejamos
2. estaríeis	teríeis estado	estai
3. estariam	teriam estado	estejam

SUBJUNCTIVE

PRESENT	IMPERFECT	FUTURE
1. esteja	estivesse	estiver
2. estejas	estivesses	estiveres
3. esteja	estivesse	estiver
1. estejamos	estivéssemos	estivermos
2. estejais	estivésseis	estiverdes
3. estejam	estivessem	estiverem

PERFECT	PLUPERFECT	FUTURE PERFECT
tenha estado etc	tivesse estado etc	tiver estado etc

INFINITIVE	*PERSONAL INFINITIVE*		*PARTICIPLE*
PRESENT estar	1. estar	1. estarmos	**PRESENT** estando
PAST ter estado	2. estares	2. estardes	**PAST** estado
	3. estar	3. estarem	

FAZER to do, to make

PRESENT	IMPERFECT	FUTURE
1. faço	fazia	farei
2. fazes	fazias	farás
3. faz	fazia	fará
1. fazemos	fazíamos	faremos
2. fazeis	fazíeis	fareis
3. fazem	faziam	farão

PRETERITE	PERFECT	PLUPERFECT
1. fiz	tenho feito	fizera
2. fizeste	tens feito	fizeras
3. fez	tem feito	fizera
1. fizemos	temos feito	fizéramos
2. fizestes	tendes feito	fizéreis
3. fizeram	têm feito	fizeram

PLUPERFECT (Compound)
tinha feito etc

FUTURE PERFECT
terei feito etc

CONDITIONAL

PRESENT	PERFECT
1. faria	teria feito
2. farias	terias feito
3. faria	teria feito
1. faríamos	teríamos feito
2. faríeis	teríeis feito
3. fariam	teriam feito

IMPERATIVE

faz
faça
façamos
fazei
façam

SUBJUNCTIVE

PRESENT	IMPERFECT	FUTURE
1. faça	fizesse	fizer
2. faças	fizesses	fizeres
3. faça	fizesse	fizer
1. façamos	fizéssemos	fizermos
2. façais	fizésseis	fizerdes
3. façam	fizessem	fizerem

PERFECT	PLUPERFECT	FUTURE PERFECT
tenha feito etc	tivesse feito etc	tiver feito etc

INFINITIVE

PRESENT fazer
PAST ter feito

PERSONAL INFINITIVE

1. fazer	1. fazermos
2. fazeres	2. fazerdes
3. fazer	3. fazerem

PARTICIPLE

PRESENT fazendo
PAST feito

HAVER to have

PRESENT	IMPERFECT	FUTURE
1. hei	havia	haverei
2. hás	havias	haverás
3. há	havia	haverá
1. havemos	havíamos	haveremos
2. haveis	havíeis	havereis
3. hão	haviam	haverão

PRETERITE	PERFECT	PLUPERFECT
1. houve	tenho havido	houvera
2. houveste	tens havido	houveras
3. houve	tem havido	houvera
1. houvemos	temos havido	houvêramos
2. houvestes	tendes havido	houvêreis
3. houveram	têm havido	houveram

PLUPERFECT (Compound)
tinha havido etc

FUTURE PERFECT
terei havido etc

CONDITIONAL

PRESENT	PERFECT	*IMPERATIVE*
1. haveria	teria havido	
2. haverias	terias havido	há
3. haveria	teria havido	haja
1. haveríamos	teríamos havido	hajamos
2. haveríeis	teríeis havido	havei
3. haveriam	teriam havido	hajam

SUBJUNCTIVE

PRESENT	IMPERFECT	FUTURE
1. haja	houvesse	houver
2. hajas	houvesses	houveres
3. haja	houvesse	houver
1. hajamos	houvéssemos	houvermos
2. hajais	houvésseis	houverdes
3. hajam	houvessem	houverem

PERFECT	PLUPERFECT	FUTURE PERFECT
tenha havido etc	tivesse havido etc	tiver havido etc

INFINITIVE
PRESENT haver
PAST ter havido

PERSONAL INFINITIVE
1. haver
2. haveres
3. haver
1. havermos
2. haverdes
3. haverem

PARTICIPLE
PRESENT havendo
PAST havido

IR to go

	PRESENT	IMPERFECT	FUTURE
1.	vou	ia	irei
2.	vais	ias	irás
3.	vai	ia	irá
1.	vamos	íamos	iremos
2.	ides	íeis	ireis
3.	vão	iam	irão

	PRETERITE	PERFECT	PLUPERFECT
1.	fui	tenho ido	fora
2.	foste	tens ido	foras
3.	foi	tem ido	fora
1.	fomos	temos ido	fôramos
2.	fostes	tendes ido	fôreis
3.	foram	têm ido	foram

PLUPERFECT (Compound)
tinha ido etc

FUTURE PERFECT
terei ido etc

CONDITIONAL

	PRESENT	PERFECT	*IMPERATIVE*
1.	iria	teria ido	
2.	irias	terias ido	vai
3.	iria	teria ido	vá
1.	iríamos	teríamos ido	vamos
2.	iríeis	teríeis ido	ide
3.	iriam	teriam ido	vão

SUBJUNCTIVE

	PRESENT	IMPERFECT	FUTURE
1.	vá	fosse	for
2.	vás	fosses	fores
3.	vá	fosse	for
1.	vamos	fôssemos	formos
2.	vades	fôsseis	fordes
3.	vão	fossem	forem

PERFECT	PLUPERFECT	FUTURE PERFECT
tenha ido etc	tivesse ido etc	tiver ido etc

INFINITIVE
PRESENT ir
PAST ter ido

PERSONAL INFINITIVE
1. ir — 1. irmos
2. ires — 2. irdes
3. ir — 3. irem

PARTICIPLE
PRESENT indo
PAST ido

PARTIR to leave; to break

PRESENT	IMPERFECT	FUTURE
1. parto	partia	partirei
2. partes	partias	partirás
3. parte	partia	partirá
1. partimos	partíamos	partiremos
2. partis	partíeis	partireis
3. partem	partiam	partirão

PRETERITE	PERFECT	PLUPERFECT
1. parti	tenho partido	partira
2. partiste	tens partido	partiras
3. partiu	tem partido	partira
1. partimos	temos partido	partíramos
2. partistes	tendes partido	partíreis
3. partiram	têm partido	partiram

PLUPERFECT (Compound)	FUTURE PERFECT
tinha partido etc	terei partido etc

CONDITIONAL / *IMPERATIVE*

PRESENT	PERFECT	IMPERATIVE
1. partiria	teria partido	
2. partirias	terias partido	parte
3. partiria	teria partido	parta
1. partiríamos	teríamos partido	partamos
2. partiríeis	teríeis partido	parti
3. partiriam	teriam partido	partam

SUBJUNCTIVE

PRESENT	IMPERFECT	FUTURE
1. parta	partisse	partir
2. partas	partisses	partires
3. parta	partisse	partir
1. partamos	partíssemos	partirmos
2. partais	partísseis	partirdes
3. partam	partissem	partirem

PERFECT	PLUPERFECT	FUTURE PERFECT
tenha partido etc	tivesse partido etc	tiver partido etc

INFINITIVE

PRESENT partir
PAST ter partido

PERSONAL INFINITIVE

1. partir	1. partirmos
2. partires	2. partirdes
3. partir	3. partirem

PARTICIPLE

PRESENT partindo
PAST partido

PODER to be able; can; to be allowed to

PRESENT	IMPERFECT	FUTURE
1. posso	podia	poderei
2. podes	podias	poderás
3. pode	podia	poderá
1. podemos	podíamos	poderemos
2. podeis	podíeis	podereis
3. podem	podiam	poderão

PRETERITE	PERFECT	PLUPERFECT
1. pude	tenho podido	pudera
2. pudeste	tens podido	puderas
3. pôde	tem podido	pudera
1. pudemos	temos podido	pudéramos
2. pudestes	tendes podido	pudéreis
3. puderam	têm podido	puderam

PLUPERFECT (Compound)
tinha podido etc

FUTURE PERFECT
terei podido etc

CONDITIONAL

PRESENT	PERFECT	*IMPERATIVE*
1. poderia	teria podido	
2. poderias	terias podido	pode
3. poderia	teria podido	possa
1. poderíamos	teríamos podido	possamos
2. poderíeis	teríeis podido	podei
3. poderiam	teriam podido	possam

SUBJUNCTIVE

PRESENT	IMPERFECT	FUTURE
1. possa	pudesse	puder
2. possas	pudesses	puderes
3. possa	pudesse	puder
1. possamos	pudéssemos	pudermos
2. possais	pudésseis	puderdes
3. possam	pudessem	puderem

PERFECT	PLUPERFECT	FUTURE PERFECT
tenha podido etc	tivesse podido etc	tiver podido etc

INFINITIVE	*PERSONAL INFINITIVE*		*PARTICIPLE*
PRESENT poder	1. poder	1. podermos	**PRESENT** podendo
PAST ter podido	2. poderes	2. poderdes	**PAST** podido
	3. poder	3. poderem	

PÔR to put, to place, to set

PRESENT	IMPERFECT	FUTURE
1. ponho	punha	porei
2. pões	punhas	porás
3. põe	punha	porá
1. pomos	púnhamos	poremos
2. pondes	púnheis	poreis
3. põem	punham	porão

PRETERITE	PERFECT	PLUPERFECT
1. pus	tenho posto	pusera
2. puseste	tens posto	puseras
3. pôs	tem posto	pusera
1. pusemos	temos posto	puséramos
2. pusestes	tendes posto	puséreis
3. puseram	têm posto	puseram

PLUPERFECT (Compound)
tinha posto etc

FUTURE PERFECT
terei posto etc

CONDITIONAL

PRESENT	PERFECT	*IMPERATIVE*
1. poria	teria posto	
2. porias	terias posto	põe
3. poria	teria posto	ponha
1. poríamos	teríamos posto	ponhamos
2. poríeis	teríeis posto	ponde
3. poriam	teriam posto	ponham

SUBJUNCTIVE

PRESENT	IMPERFECT	FUTURE
1. ponha	pusesse	puser
2. ponhas	pusesses	puseres
3. ponha	pusesse	puser
1. ponhamos	puséssemos	pusermos
2. ponhais	pusésseis	puserdes
3. ponham	pusessem	puserem

PERFECT	PLUPERFECT	FUTURE PERFECT
tenha posto etc	tivesse posto etc	tiver posto etc

INFINITIVE	*PERSONAL INFINITIVE*		*PARTICIPLE*
PRESENT pôr	1. pôr	1. pormos	**PRESENT** pondo
PAST ter posto	2. pores	2. pordes	**PAST** posto
	3. pôr	3. porem	

SENTAR-SE to sit

PRESENT	IMPERFECT	FUTURE
1. sento-me	sentava-me	sentar-me-ei
2. sentas-te	sentavas-te	sentar-te-ás
3. senta-se	sentava-se	sentar-se-á
1. sentamo-nos	sentávamo-nos	sentar-nos-emos
2. sentais-vos	sentáveis-vos	sentar-vos-eis
3. sentam-se	sentavam-se	sentar-se-ão

PRETERITE	PERFECT	PLUPERFECT
1. sentei-me	tenho-me sentado	sentara-me
2. sentaste-te	tens-te sentado	sentaras-te
3. sentou-se	tem-se sentado	sentara-se
1. sentámo-nos	temo-nos sentado	sentáramo-nos
2. sentastes-vos	tendes-vos sentado	sentáreis-vos
3. sentaram-se	têm-se sentado	sentaram-se

PLUPERFECT (Compound)
tinha-me sentado etc

FUTURE PERFECT
ter-me-ei sentado etc

CONDITIONAL

PRESENT	PERFECT	*IMPERATIVE*
1. sentar-me-ia	ter-me-ia sentado	
2. sentar-te-ias	ter-te-ias sentado	senta-te
3. sentar-se-ia	ter-se-ia sentado	sente-se
1. sentar-nos-íamos	ter-nos-íamos sentado	sentemo-nos
2. sentar-vos-íeis	ter-vos-íeis sentado	sentai-vos
3. sentar-se-iam	ter-se-iam sentado	sentem-se

SUBJUNCTIVE

PRESENT	IMPERFECT	FUTURE
1. me sente	me sentasse	me sentar
2. te sentes	te sentasses	te sentares
3. se sente	se sentasse	se sentar
1. nos sentemos	nos sentássemos	nos sentarmos
2. vos senteis	vos sentásseis	vos sentardes
3. se sentem	se sentassem	se sentarem

PERFECT	PLUPERFECT	FUTURE PERFECT
me tenha sentado etc	me tivesse sentado etc	me tiver sentado etc

INFINITIVE

PRESENT sentar-se
PAST ter-se sentado

PERSONAL INFINITIVE

1. me sentar
2. te sentares
3. se sentar
1. nos sentarmos
2. vos sentardes
3. se sentarem

PARTICIPLE

PRESENT sentando-se
PAST sentado

SER to be

PRESENT	IMPERFECT	FUTURE
1. sou	era	serei
2. és	eras	serás
3. é	era	será
1. somos	éramos	seremos
2. sois	éreis	sereis
3. são	eram	serão

PRETERITE	PERFECT	PLUPERFECT
1. fui	tenho sido	fora
2. foste	tens sido	foras
3. foi	tem sido	fora
1. fomos	temos sido	fôramos
2. fostes	tendes sido	fôreis
3. foram	têm sido	foram

PLUPERFECT (Compound)
tinha sido etc

FUTURE PERFECT
terei sido etc

CONDITIONAL

PRESENT	PERFECT	*IMPERATIVE*
1. seria	teria sido	
2. serias	terias sido	sê
3. seria	teria sido	seja
1. seríamos	teríamos sido	sejamos
2. seríeis	teríeis sido	sede
3. seriam	teriam sido	sejam

SUBJUNCTIVE

PRESENT	IMPERFECT	FUTURE
1. seja	fosse	for
2. sejas	fosses	fores
3. seja	fosse	for
1. sejamos	fôssemos	formos
2. sejais	fôsseis	fordes
3. sejam	fossem	forem

PERFECT	PLUPERFECT	FUTURE PERFECT
tenha sido etc	tivesse sido etc	tiver sido etc

INFINITIVE
PRESENT ser
PAST ter sido

PERSONAL INFINITIVE
1. ser
2. seres
3. ser
1. sermos
2. serdes
3. serem

PARTICIPLE
PRESENT sendo
PAST sido

TER to have

PRESENT	IMPERFECT	FUTURE
1. tenho	tinha	terei
2. tens	tinhas	terás
3. tem	tinha	terá
1. temos	tínhamos	teremos
2. tendes	tínheis	tereis
3. têm	tinham	terão

PRETERITE	PERFECT	PLUPERFECT
1. tive	tenho tido	tivera
2. tiveste	tens tido	tiveras
3. teve	tem tido	tivera
1. tivemos	temos tido	tivéramos
2. tivestes	tendes tido	tivéreis
3. tiveram	têm tido	tiveram

PLUPERFECT (Compound)
tinha tido etc

FUTURE PERFECT
terei tido etc

CONDITIONAL

PRESENT	PERFECT	*IMPERATIVE*
1. teria	teria tido	
2. terias	terias tido	tem
3. teria	teria tido	tenha
1. teríamos	teríamos tido	tenhamos
2. teríeis	teríeis tido	tende
3. teriam	teriam tido	tenham

SUBJUNCTIVE

PRESENT	IMPERFECT	FUTURE
1. tenha	tivesse	tiver
2. tenhas	tivesses	tiveres
3. tenha	tivesse	tiver
1. tenhamos	tivéssemos	tivermos
2. tenhais	tivésseis	tiverdes
3. tenham	tivessem	tiverem

PERFECT	PLUPERFECT	FUTURE PERFECT
tenha tido etc	tivesse tido etc	tiver tido etc

INFINITIVE
PRESENT ter
PAST ter tido

PERSONAL INFINITIVE

1. ter	1. termos
2. teres	2. terdes
3. ter	3. terem

PARTICIPLE
PRESENT tendo
PAST tido

VER to see

PRESENT	IMPERFECT	FUTURE
1. vejo	via	verei
2. vês	vias	verás
3. vê	via	verá
1. vemos	víamos	veremos
2. vedes	víeis	vereis
3. vêem	viam	verão

PRETERITE	PERFECT	PLUPERFECT
1. vi	tenho visto	vira
2. viste	tens visto	viras
3. viu	tem visto	vira
1. vimos	temos visto	víramos
2. vistes	tendes visto	víreis
3. viram	têm visto	viram

PLUPERFECT (Compound)
tinha visto etc

FUTURE PERFECT
terei visto etc

CONDITIONAL

PRESENT	PERFECT	*IMPERATIVE*
1. veria	teria visto	
2. verias	terias visto	vê
3. veria	teria visto	veja
1. veríamos	teríamos visto	vejamos
2. veríeis	teríeis visto	vede
3. veriam	teriam visto	vejam

SUBJUNCTIVE

PRESENT	IMPERFECT	FUTURE
1. veja	visse	vir
2. vejas	visses	vires
3. veja	visse	vir
1. vejamos	víssemos	virmos
2. vejais	vísseis	virdes
3. vejam	vissem	virem

PERFECT	PLUPERFECT	FUTURE PERFECT
tenha visto etc	tivesse visto etc	tiver visto etc

INFINITIVE

PRESENT ver
PAST ter visto

PERSONAL INFINITIVE

1. ver	1. vermos
2. veres	2. verdes
3. ver	3. verem

PARTICIPLE

PRESENT vendo
PAST visto

VIR to come

PRESENT	IMPERFECT	FUTURE
1. venho	vinha	virei
2. vens	vinhas	virás
3. vem	vinha	virá
1. vimos	vínhamos	viremos
2. vindes	vínheis	vireis
3. vêm	vinham	virão

PRETERITE	PERFECT	PLUPERFECT
1. vim	tenho vindo	viera
2. vieste	tens vindo	vieras
3. veio	tem vindo	viera
1. viemos	temos vindo	viéramos
2. viestes	tendes vindo	viéreis
3. vieram	têm vindo	vieram

PLUPERFECT (Compound)
tinha vindo etc

FUTURE PERFECT
terei vindo etc

CONDITIONAL

PRESENT	PERFECT	*IMPERATIVE*
1. viria	teria vindo	
2. virias	terias vindo	vem
3. viria	teria vindo	venha
1. viríamos	teríamos vindo	venhamos
2. viríeis	teríeis vindo	vinde
3. viriam	teriam vindo	venham

SUBJUNCTIVE

PRESENT	IMPERFECT	FUTURE
1. venha	viesse	vier
2. venhas	viesses	vieres
3. venha	viesse	vier
1. venhamos	viéssemos	viermos
2. venhais	viésseis	vierdes
3. venham	viessem	vierem

PERFECT	PLUPERFECT	FUTURE PERFECT
tenha vindo etc	tivesse vindo etc	tiver vindo etc

INFINITIVE
PRESENT vir
PAST ter vindo

PERSONAL INFINITIVE
1. vir	1. virmos
2. vires	2. virdes
3. vir	3. virem

PARTICIPLE
PRESENT vindo
PAST vindo

9. PREPOSITIONS

Prepositions are those words generally indicating place, time, manner and movement that serve to clarify the relationship between other words (nouns, pronouns, verbs and adverbs).

A. SIMPLE PREPOSITIONS

a	at, to
antes	before
após	after
até	up to, until
com	with
contra	against
de	of, from, about
desde	since, from
em	in, on, at
entre	between, among
para	for, to, toward
por	for, by, through
sem	without
sob	below, under
sobre	on, on top of, about

está no cinema
he's at the cinema

com quem?
who with?

estamos em Lisboa
we are in Lisbon

saiu sem o dinheiro
she went out without her money

dia após dia
day after day

foi para Lisboa
he went to Lisbon

For a fuller explanation of **para** and **por** and their differences, see page 174.

B. COMPOUND PREPOSITIONS

à frente (de)	at the front (of)
além (de)	beyond, besides
antes (de)	before
ao redor (de)	around
atrás (de)	behind
através (de)	through, across
à volta (de)	around, about
debaixo (de)	under
defronte (de)	opposite
dentro (de)	inside
depois (de)	after
detrás (de)	behind
em cima (de)	on top of
em frente (de)	in front of
em volta (de)	around, about
fora (de)	outside
longe (de)	far (from)
perto (de)	near, nearby
por cima (de)	over, above
por dentro (de)	(from) inside
por volta (de)	around, about

The word **de** is used when the preposition is followed by other words (nouns, verbs, pronouns). When it is followed by articles and demonstratives, it combines and contracts with them. See page 173.

à frente da casa há um rio
at the front of the house there is a river

fomos através da ponte
we went across the bridge

o que há dentro do saco?
what is there inside the bag?

o banco fica em frente da praça
the bank is in front of the square

fica perto?
is it nearby?

além de peixe, também comprou leite
as well as fish, she also bought milk

C. VERBS WITH PREPOSITIONS

As well as those verbs discussed on page 144, which take on specific meanings when followed by a preposition, verbs in the infinitive may also be preceded by prepositions.

além de trabalhar, também estuda à noite
as well as working, he also studies at night

antes de sair, vou preparar o jantar
before going out I'm going to prepare dinner

depois de fazermos o bolo, vamos comê-lo?
after making the cake, shall we eat it?

Constructions using a preposition + **que** + verb, form what is known as a *compound conjunction*. These often call for a subjunctive verb form.

paguei a multa para que o meu marido não soubesse do acidente
I paid the fine so that my husband wouldn't find out about the accident

D. PREPOSITIONS OF TIME

a) **a** at/on

Used with: dates with a day of the month, time, parts of the day, days of the week (when talking about usual habits)

o dia de Natal é a 25 de Dezembro
christmas Day is on the 25th December

a biblioteca fecha às cinco horas
the library closes at 5 o'clock

a reunião é à tarde
the meeting is in the afternoon

nunca vou ao centro às sextas
I never go to town on Fridays

b) **de** from/of

Used with: dates, parts of the day, times

a minha data de nascimento é o 15 de Setembro [BP setembro] de 1965.
my date of birth is the 15th of September, 1965.

o avião chega às 8 horas da manhã
the plane arrives at 8 o'clock in the morning

o mercado abre das 06.30 às 15.30
the market opens from 6.30 until 15.30

c) **em** in/on/at

Used with: dates (with the word 'day'), months, days of the week (specific), years, special festivities, centuries, seasons

as aulas começam no dia 12
classes start on the 12th

sempre chove em Abril [BP abril]
it always rains in April

na quarta (-feira) vou ao teatro
on Wednesday I'm going to the theatre

fomos para a França em 1996
we went to France in 1996

comemos ovos de chocolate na Páscoa
we eat chocolate eggs at Easter

morreu no século 19
he died in the 19th century

no Inverno gosto de ir esquiar
in Winter I like going skiing

d) Other expressions

i) **antes de** before

ela chegou antes do irmão
she arrived before her brother

temos de partir antes das sete
we have to leave before seven

ii) **à/por volta de, por, lá para [BP]** about/around

venha por volta das 8
come about 8 o'clock

começa pelas onze horas
it begins around 11

chegámos [BP chegamos] lá para meia-noite
we arrived at about midnight

iii) **depois de, após** after

a loja abre só depois das dez
the shop only opens after ten

a chuva continua, dia após dia
the rain continues, day after day

iv) **desde... até** from... until

a viagem levou desde as cinco até às oito e meia
the journey took from 5 until 8.30

as lojas abrem desde as sete até ao meio-dia
the shops open from 7 until midday

E. CONTRACTIONS

The following prepositions combine and contract with definite and indefinite articles and demonstratives.

a	+ definite article	= **ao/à/aos/às**
em	+ definite article	= **no/na/nos/nas**
	+ indefinite article	= **num/numa/nuns/numas**
	+ demonstrative	= **neste(s)/nesta(s)/nisto**
		nesse(s)/nessa(s)/nisso
		naquele(s)/naquela(s)/naquilo
de	+ definite article	= **do/da/dos/das**
	+ indefinite article	= **dum/duma/duns/dumas**
	+ demonstrative	= **deste(s)/desta(s)/disto**
		desse(s)/dessa(s)/disso
		daquele(s)/daquela(s)/daquilo
por	+ definite article	= **pelo/pela/pelos/pelas**

fomos ao supermercado
we went to the supermarket

mora numa casa antiga
she lives in an old house

gosto mais deste livro
I like this book best

vão passar pelas praças
they are going to pass through the squares

Other contractions, such as **de** + **algum** > **dalgum**, exist, but can be used in the written language as two separate words, although sometimes pronounced as one when spoken.

F. POR AND PARA

The prepositions **por** and **para** can cause some confusion, as their varied meanings sometimes overlap. **Por** contracts with the definite article to form **pelo**, (**-a**, **-os**, **-as**).

POR

Por ("for", "through", "by", "along", "per", "because of") is used in the following situations:

a) Place through, by, along or near

fomos um passeio pelo parque
we went a stroll through the park

o comboio [BP trem] passa por minha escola
the train passes near my school

b) Expressions of time – through, during, for, around

falaram pela tarde fora
they talked throughout the whole afternoon

vamos a Angola por quinze dias
we are going to Angola for a fortnight

volto pelas 8 horas
I'll be back around 8 o'clock

c) Exchange, price for, substitution for

quanto pagou por esse vestido?
how much did you pay for that dress?

vou trocar o carro por outro mais novo
I'm going to change my car for a newer one

d) Unit of measure, by, per, frequency

50 quilómetros por hora
50 km an hour

5 euros por quilo
5 euros a kilo

vou ao ginásio três vezes por semana
I go to the gym 3 times a week

e) Way or means by, through

posso mandar esta carta por avião?
can I send this letter by airmail?

ela soube da festa pelo João
she found out about the party through João

f) Because of, on account of, for

foi demitida pelo comportamento
she was sacked because of her behaviour

Portugal é conhecido pelo sol e pelas boas praias
Portugal is well known for its sun and good beaches

g) To go for, send for something

foi ao mercado por cenouras
he went to the market for some carrots

mandaram-no aos correios por selos
they sent him to the post office for stamps

h) On behalf of, for the sake of, for

este ano não votei por partido nenhum
this year I didn't vote for any party

falou por todos quando disse...
he spoke for everyone when he said...

i) Motive, reason for

levou o dinheiro por necessidade
he took the money by necessity

morreram todos por falta de ar
they all died through a lack of air

j) On the occasion of

no Brasil, é comum festejar na praia pelo Reveillon
in Brazil it's common to celebrate on the beach on New Year's Eve

k) In the passive voice, to introduce the agent – "by" (see page 134)

eu fui picado por um escorpião
I was bitten by a scorpion

as janelas foram partidas por aqueles meninos
the windows were broken by those boys

PARA

Para ("for", "to", "in order to", "towards") is used in the following situations:

a) Use, for

esta é uma faca para cortar pão
this is a bread knife (a knife for cutting bread)

há tudo aqui para fazer bolos
there is everything here for making cakes

b) Destination (place or person) towards, for/direction

partiram para a Nova York
they departed for New York

isto é para a minha mãe
this is for my mother

vou para o norte
I'm going to the north

c) Purpose, in order to

telefonei-lhe para o convidar ao baile
I phoned him to invite him to the dance

fui ao centro para comprar uma prenda
I went to town (in order) to buy a present

d) Time expressions, for, by, towards

pode fazê-lo para o Sábado?
can you do it by Saturday?

as férias começam lá para o fim de Julho [BP julho]
the holidays begin towards the end of July

e) Comparison – for me, for him, etc

isto é importante para mim, mas não para eles
this is important for me, but not for them

10. CONJUNCTIONS

Conjunctions are parts of speech that link words, phrases or clauses.

A. SIMPLE CONJUNCTIONS

Simple conjunctions consist of one word only. The most common are:

caso	in case
como	as (reason)
conforme	as
conquanto	although
e	and
embora	although
enquanto	while
mas	but
mesmo	even, although
nem	neither/nor
ou	or
porque	because
pois	as, since, because
quando	when
que	that, for (because)
se	if, whether
segundo	according to
senão	but

embora esteja cansado, vou ver o filme
although I'm tired, I'm going to watch the film

fui ver o meu primo, mas não estava em casa
I went to see my cousin, but he wasn't at home

compramos um bilhete porque queremos ganhar
we buy a ticket because we want to win

não sei se posso trabalhar
I don't know if I can work

mesmo estando cansado, o Paulo fez o jantar
even though he was tired, Paulo made the dinner

queres ir nadar ou jogar ténis?
do you want to go swimming, or to play tennis?

B. COMPOUND CONJUNCTIONS

These conjunctions consist of two or more words, the last one often being **que**. Many of these expressions take the subjunctive after them. See page 113.

a fim de que	in order that
ainda quando	even if
ainda que	although
ainda se	even if
a menos que	unless
a não ser que	unless
antes que	before
assim que	as soon as
até que	until
(no) caso que	in case
contanto que	provided that, since
dado que	given that
desde que	provided that
logo que	as soon as
mesmo que	even if
nem que	not even if
para que	in order that
posto que	although
primeiro que	before
se bem que	although
sem que	without
sempre que	whenever
sob condição que	on condition that

tens que estudar mais a fim de que obtenhas boas notas
you have to study more in order to get good marks

ainda que estivesse doente, ajudou-me com o trabalho
even though he was ill, he helped me with the work

até que estejas melhor, não deverias sair
until you are better, you shouldn't go out

desde que não seja inconveniente, vamos passar aí no sábado
provided it's not inconvenient, we'll pass by there on Saturday

toma nota do número para que não o esquece
note down the number so that you don't forget it

sem que se abra a lata, não se pode ver o que é
without opening the tin, you can't see what it is

C. COORDINATING CONJUNCTIONS

Coordinating conjunctions come in pairs and are used to link two closely associated ideas:

apenas...quando	hardly...when
não...mas (sim)	not...but
não só...mas também	not only...but also
nem...nem	neither...nor
ou...ou	either...or
tanto...como	not only...but also (both... and)

ela comprou não só laranjas, mas também pêras
she not only bought oranges, but pears too

ou você ajude o seu pai ou limpe o quarto
either help your father or clean your room

tanto os meus amigos como os meus irmãos vão fazer a maratona
not only my friends but also my brothers are going to do the marathon

D. DIRECT AND INDIRECT SPEECH

Direct speech is where the exact words of the speaker are recorded, in whatever tense that may be, with the punctuation of speech marks to indicate that this is a replica of the original statement. Indirect speech, on the other hand, is often referred to as 'reported speech', as it is a report of what was said, and is preceded by expressions such as: she said that..., they suggested that... . It is important when moving from direct to indirect speech to take into account tenses, pronouns, prepositions and adverbs of place and time, as all of these may need to change.

The following comparison may help to illustrate examples of some of the changes between the two forms of speech:

	Direct Speech	Indirect Speech
Punctuation	Speech marks or question marks/ exclamation marks	None
Verbs of speech	Verbs such as: **contar, dizer, responder, sugerir, saber, etc**	Same range of verbs, followed by **que, se** or **para**
Tense/Mood	Present Indicative Preterite Future Present Subjunctive Imperfect Subj.	Imperfect Indicative Pluperfect Conditional Imperfect Subjunctive Imperfect Subj.

	Future Subjunctive Imperative	Imperfect Subj. Imperfect Subj. or Infinitive
Pronouns/ Possessives		Changes may occur to all
Demonstratives	**este/esse, etc** **isto/isso**	**aquele, etc** **aquilo**
Adverbs of Place	**aqui** **cá** **neste lugar, etc**	**ali** **lá** **naquele lugar, etc**
Adverbs of Time	**ontem** **hoje** **amanhã** **agora** **no próximo mês**	**no dia anterior** **nesse dia/naquele dia** **no dia seguinte** **naquele momento** **no mês seguinte**

"vou à casa da minha prima", disse a Maria
"I'm going to my cousin's house", said Maria

a Maria disse que ia à casa da prima (dela)
Maria said that she was going to her cousin's house

a festa não foi boa; não me deram prendas – contou o Luís
the party wasn't any good; they didn't give me any presents – Luis said

Luís contou que a festa não tinha sido boa, e que não lhe tinham dado prendas
Luis said that the party hadn't been any good and that they hadn't given him any presents

"liga a televisão!", pediu-me o meu avô
"put the TV on", my grandfather asked me

o meu avô pediu-me que ligasse a televisão OR pediu-me para ligar...
my grandfather asked me to put the TV on

"a semana passada os meus primos passaram dois dias cá em casa", disse a Paula
"last week my cousins spent two days here at home", said Paula

a Paula disse que na semana anterior, os primos (dela) tinham passado dois dias lá na casa dela
Paula said that in the previous week, her cousins had spent two days there at her home

quem quer ir à discoteca? – pediu
who wants to go to the disco?, she asked

pediu quem queria ir à discoteca
she asked who wanted to go to the disco

11. NUMBERS AND QUANTITY

A. CARDINAL NUMBERS

0	zero
1	um, uma
2	dois, duas
3	três
4	quatro
5	cinco
6	seis
7	sete
8	oito
9	nove
10	dez
11	onze
12	doze
13	treze
14	catorze [BP quatorze]
15	quinze
16	dezasseis [BP dezesseis]
17	dezassete [BP dezessete]
18	dezoito
19	dezanove [BP dezenove]
20	vinte
21	vinte e um/uma
22	vinte e dois/duas
23	vinte e três

24	vinte e quatro
25	vinte e cinco
30	trinta
31	trinta e um/uma
32	trinta e dois/duas
40	quarenta
50	cinquenta [BP cinqüenta]
60	sessenta
70	setenta
80	oitenta
90	noventa
100	cem, cento
101	cento e um/uma
110	cento e dez
200	duzentos,(as)
300	trezentos,(as)
400	quatrocentos,(as)
500	quinhentos,(as)
600	seiscentos,(as)
700	setecentos,(as)
800	oitocentos,(as)
900	novecentos,(as)
1,000	mil
2,000	dois mil
100,000	cem mil
1,000,000	um milhão
2,000,000	dois milhões
1,000,000,000	mil milhões

In Brazil, um **bilhão** is equivalent to one billion (1, followed by nine zeros).

a) Numbers one and two have both masculine and feminine forms, which are retained whenever those numerals appear.

vinte e duas cervejas
22 beers

cento e uma cadeiras
101 chairs

b) Numbers in the hundreds also have two forms:

trezentas milhas
300 miles

quinhentas libras
500 pounds

c) Above one thousand, numbers are always expressed in thousands and hundreds, and not as multiples of a hundred (as in the English "twelve hundred and fifty"), hence the year 1752 is **mil**, **setecentos e cinquenta e dois**.

The word **e** ("and") appears between hundreds, tens and single digits.

cento e oitenta e dois
182

d) **E** appears after thousands in the following circumstances only:

i) When the thousand is followed directly by a numeral from 1–100.

sete mil e oitenta e cinco
7,085

ii) When the thousand is followed by a numeral from 200–999, if the last two numbers are zeros.

vinte e cinco mil e trezentos
25,300

e) In Portuguese, a full stop is inserted after thousands, etc, instead of a comma. Hence 1,532 is written 1.532, and 252,000 is 252.000.

f) "A" is not translated before **cem**, **cento** or **mil**.

cem libras
(a) hundred pounds

mil dólares
(a) thousand dollars

B. ORDINAL NUMBERS

1st	**primeiro (-a,-os,-as)**
2nd	**segundo**
3rd	**terceiro**
4th	**quarto**
5th	**quinto**
6th	**sexto**
7th	**sétimo**
8th	**oitavo**
9th	**nono**
10th	**décimo**
11th	**décimo primeiro**
12th	**décimo segundo**
13th	**décimo terceiro**
14th	**décimo quarto**

15th	**décimo quinto**
16th	**décimo sexto**
17th	**décimo sétimo**
18th	**décimo oitavo**
19th	**décimo nono**
20th	**vigésimo**
21st	**vigésimo primeiro**
22nd	**vigésimo segundo**
30th	**trigésimo**
40th	**quadragésimo**
50th	**quinquagésimo [BP qüinquagésimo]**
60th	**sexagésimo**
70th	**septuagésimo [BP setuagésimo]**
80th	**octagésimo**
90th	**nonagésimo**
100th	**centésimo**
1000th	**milésimo**

a) Ordinals may be abbreviated by using the appropriate number, plus the last vowel of the number (**o** or **a**). This is clearly seen in addresses:

mora no 15° (décimo quinto) andar
she lives on the 15th floor

b) Ordinals agree in number and gender with the noun to which they refer. In the compound versions (**décimo primeiro**, **décimo segundo**, **vigésimo primeiro**, etc), both parts of the number agree.

a décima segunda janela
the twelfth window

c) Ordinals are not used very frequently in Portuguese beyond tenth, except in addresses (particularly for the number of the floor in apartment blocks).

fica no décimo oitavo andar
it's on the eighteenth floor

d) In reference to popes, royalty and centuries, ordinals are used up to tenth, and from there on cardinal numbers are introduced. In both cases, the numbers follow the titles.

João Primeiro
John the First

o século quinto
the fifth century

Manuel Doze
Manuel the Twelfth

o Século Vinte e Um
the twenty-first century

C. MATHEMATICAL EXPRESSIONS

a) Arithmetical Signs

somar to add up	**adição** addition	+	**e/mais** and
subtrair to take away	**subtracção** subtraction	-	**menos** minus
multiplicar to multiply	**multiplicação** multiplication	x	**vezes/multiplicado por** times/multiplied by
dividir to divide	**divisão** division	÷	**dividido por** divided by
calcular to calculate		=	**são/dá/dão/é igual a** are/give(s)/equals

3+2=5	**três mais dois são cinco**
9-6=3	**nove menos seis dão três**
3x3=9	**três vezes três são nove**
10÷2=5	**dez dividido por dois dá cinco**

b) Fractions

1/2	**um meio**
1/3	**um terço**
1/4	**um quarto**
3/4	**três quartos**
1/5	**um quinto**
1/6	**um sexto**
1/7	**um sétimo**
1/8	**um oitavo**
1/9	**um nono**
1/10	**um décimo**

c) Decimals

In Portuguese, the decimal point is represented by a comma, and not a full stop. Hence, 4.8 is written as 4,8 and 0.001 is 0,001. The comma is subsequently part of the decimal as it is written or spoken in full.

4,8 = **quatro vírgula oito**
0,001 = **zero vírgula zero zero um**

D. MEASUREMENTS AND PRICES

a) **Ter** (to have), **ser** (to be), **medir** (to measure) and **pesar** (to weigh) are verbs used in measurements.

Nouns		Adjectives
a altura/a elevação	height	**alto**
o comprimento/ a extensão	length	**comprido/longo**
a largura	width	**largo**
a profundidade	depth	**profundo**
a grossura	thickness	**grosso**
o peso	weight	**pesado**

a sala tem três metros de comprimento e dois de largura
the room is three metres long by two metres wide

o mar tem duas braças de profundidade
the sea is two fathoms deep

a casa mede sete metros de elevação
the house is seven metres tall

b) Units of Measure, Metric System

quilómetro*	**hectómetro**	
km	**hm**	
decâmetro	**metro**	
dam	**m**	
decímetro	**centímetro**	**milímetro**
dm	**cm**	**mm**
quilograma	**hectograma**	
kg	**hg**	
decagrama	**grama**	
dag	**g**	
decigrama	**centigrama**	**miligrama**
dg	**cg**	**mg**
quilolitro	**hectolitro**	
kl	**hl**	
decalitro	**litro**	
dal	**l**	
decilitro	**centilitro**	**mililitro**
dl	**cl**	**ml**

***[BP quilômetro]**

Area/Volume:
$1m^2$= um metro quadrado
$4m^2$= quatro metros quadrados
$1m^3$ = um metro cúbico
$5m^3$ = cinco metros cúbicos

c) Other Units of Measurement

a polegada	inch
o pé	foot
a jarda	yard
a milha	mile
o quartilho	pint
um galão	gallon
a libra	pound
a tonelada	ton

d) Geometrical Terms

o ângulo	angle
o ângulo agudo	acute angle
o ângulo obtuso	obtuse angle
o ângulo recto [BP reto]	right angle
o círculo	circle
o diâmetro	diameter
a linha	line
o perímetro	perimeter
o polígano	polygon
o quadrado	square
o raio	radius
o rectângulo	rectangle
o rombóide	rhomboid
o triângulo	triangle

e) Solids

o cilindro	cylinder
o cone	cone
o cubo	cube
a esfera	sphere
o hemisfério	hemisphere
a pirâmide	pyramid
o prisma	prism

f) Other measurement language

a amplitude	space/extent
a área	area
o dobro	double
maior	greater/bigger
a medida	measurement
menor	lesser/smaller
a metade	half
a quantidade	quantity
o recipiente	container
uma régua	ruler
o valor	value
a velocidade	speed

g) Prices

qual é o preço dum quarto individual?
what is the price of a single room?

quanto custa/é uma garrafa de vinho?
how much is a bottle of wine?

custa/é 1 euro por garrafa
it's 1 euro a bottle

quanto custam/são dois quilos de laranjas?
how much/are two kilos of oranges?

custam/são 2 euros
they cost/are 2 euros

a quanto estão as maçãs?
what's the price of the apples/what price have you got your apples at?

quanto custa/é ao todo/em total?
how much does it cost/is it in all/in total?

são 4 euros ao todo
that's 4 euros altogether

E. EXPRESSIONS OF QUANTITY

1. Adverbs, adjectives and pronouns of quantity

um/uma/uns/umas
a, one, some

quanto/a/os/as
how much, many

muito/a/os/as (de)
much, many, a lot (of)

pouco/a/os/as (de)
little, few (of)

um pouco/pouquinho (de)
a little, bit, some (of)

vários/as
several

demais, demasiado
too much

suficiente/s
enough, sufficient

tanto/a/os/as
so much, so many

tanto/a/os/as... quanto/a/os/as
as much, many...as

menos	**mais**	**suficiente**	**bastante**
less, fewer	more	enough	quite (enough)

a maior parte (de)/a maioria (de)
most, the majority (of)

não tenho muito tempo
I haven't much time

tenho bastante trabalho
I have quite a lot of work

queria um pouco de açúcar
I'd like a bit of sugar

poucos vieram
few came

têm tantos problemas
they have so many problems

quantas malas leva?
how many cases are you taking?

temos mais experiência
we have more experience

hoje há menos aviões
today there are fewer planes

tem dinheiro suficiente?
do you have enough money?

a maioria das pessoas
most people

2. Nouns expressing quantity

uma caixa de
a box of

uma garrafa de
a bottle of

um garrafão de
a demi-john of

um pote de
a pot/jar of

um tubo de
a tube of

uma dose de
a portion of

uma lata de
a tin/can of

um frasco de
a jar of

um bocado de
a mouthful/a bit of

um pacote de
a packet of

um rolo de
a roll of

um conjunto de
a set of

uma colherada de
a spoonful of

um quilo de
a kilo of

meio quilo/litro de
half a kilo/litre of

uma porção de
a portion of

uma chávena [BP xícara] de
a cup of

um pedaço/pedacinho de
a piece/little piece of

um litro de
a litre of

um par de
a pair of

uma fatia de
a slice of

um copo de
a glass of

queria uma lata de tomates e um litro de azeite
I would like a tin of tomatoes and a litre of (olive) oil

precisa de um quilo e meio de farinha
you need a kilo and a half of flour

vou comprar um par de sapatos
I'm going to buy a pair of shoes

12. EXPRESSIONS OF TIME

A. THE TIME

i) Time of Day

que horas são?
what time is it?

que horas eram?
what time was it?

tem as horas?
do you have the time?

é a uma (hora)
It's one o'clock

são duas (horas)
it's two o'clock

é meio-dia
it's midday

era meia-noite
it was midnight

ii) Time past the hour is denoted by adding the number of minutes, up to thirty, on to the hour, using the word **e** (and). If it is midday, midnight, or any time connected to one o'clock, you start the sentence with **é** (it is). For hours beyond that (2 onwards), use **são** (they are), because you are dealing with hours in the plural.

são quatro e dez
it's ten past four

é uma e um quarto (quinze)
it's a quarter past one (one fifteen)

são cinco e meia (trinta)
it's half past five

iii) Time up to the hour can be expressed in three ways:

1. By subtracting the minutes from the nearest next full hour, using **menos**

são oito menos dez
it's ten to eight

é meio-dia menos um quarto
it's a quarter to twelve (midday)

2. By using the number of minutes to the hour + **para**

são vinte para as seis
it's twenty to six

é um quarto para a uma
it's a quarter to one

3. With **faltar** (to be lacking) + the number of minutes to the hour + **para**

faltam quinze para as três
it's a quarter to three

faltam dez para meia-noite
it's ten to midnight

iv) **A que horas...?** At what time...?

a que horas parte/chega o autocarro [BP ônibus]?
at what time does the bus depart/arrive?

a que horas abre/ fecha o mercado?
at what time does the market open/ close?

a que horas começa/termina o baile?
at what time does the dance start/finish?

à uma hora
at one o'clock

ao meio-dia/à meia-noite
at midday/at midnight

And for hours beyond one:

às quatro (horas)
at four (o'clock)

às três e meia
at 3.30

às oito menos vinte
at 7.40

às dez para as seis
at ten to six

(**faltar** is not used here)

v) The twenty-four hour clock, commonly used in timetables, is often more straightforward, as you simply deal with the numbers in the order they appear.

o avião parte às vinte e duas e quarenta
the plane leaves at 22:40

o barco chega às quinze e vinte e nove
the boat arrives at 15:29

vi) To talk about time from…until…, use the prepositions **de** and **a**

da uma/do meio-dia/da meia-noite
from one o'clock/from midday/from midnight

das quatro (horas)
from 4 (o'clock)

à uma/ao meio-dia/à meia-noite
'til one/to midday/to midnight

às sete
to/'til seven

às oito e meia
to/'til 8.30

vii) You can also use the word **até** (until) in these expressions:

das oito até às nove
from 8 until 9

viii) **A partir de** (from...) is also used, especially if there is a set starting time for things such as mealtimes in hotels, or events:

servimos o pequeno-almoço [BP café da manhã] a partir das sete horas
we serve breakfast from 7 (onwards)

os preços aumentam a partir de Junho
prices go up from June

B. DATE

a) Days of the Week – **os dias da semana**

(a) segunda-feira	Monday
(a) terça-feira	Tuesday
(a) quarta-feira	Wednesday
(a) quinta-feira	Thursday
(a) sexta-feira	Friday
(o) sábado	Saturday
(o) domingo	Sunday

Weekdays are feminine, and it is common in the spoken language to drop the **-feira** suffix from each one. The days of the weekend are masculine. There appears to be little consensus as to whether they are written with a capital letter or not.

The prepositions **em** and **a** are used with days of the week.

na sexta-feira
on Friday

nas quintas
on Thursdays

o barco parte às quartas e às sextas
the boat departs on Wednesdays and Fridays

partimos no Sábado
we depart on Saturday

amanhã é domingo
tomorrow is Sunday

todos os domingos eles vão à missa
they go to Mass every Sunday

segunda de manhã, vai ao hospital
on Monday morning he's going to hospital

b) Months of the Year – **os meses do ano**

Janeiro January
Fevereiro February
Março March
Abril April
Maio May
Junho June
Julho July
Agosto August
Setembro September
Outubro October
Novembro November
Dezembro December

c) Seasons of the Year – **as estações do ano**

a Primavera spring
o Verão summer

o Outono autumn
o Inverno winter

[Note that in Brazilian Portuguese capital letters are generally not used for months or seasons]

d) Special Holidays – **férias/feriados** (bank or national holidays)

a Passagem do Ano/o Reveillon	New Year's Eve
o Ano Novo	New Year
o Carnaval	Carnival
a Quaresma	Lent
a Páscoa	Easter
o Natal	Christmas

e) Dates

Cardinal numbers (one, two, three, etc) are used with dates, including the first – **(o dia) um**. However, the 1st January is usually still referred to as **o Primeiro de Janeiro** = New Year's Day.

que data é hoje?
what date is it today?

quantos são hoje?
what is the date today?

a quantos estamos?
what's the date? [lit. At what (day) are we]

é o dia vinte e nove
it's the twenty-ninth

hoje são dezassete
it's the seventeenth today

estamos a vinte e oito
it's the twenty-eighth

estávamos a/no dia 21 de Maio
it was the 21st May

é o dia vinte e um de Setembro
it's the twenty-first of September

nasceu a doze de Agosto de 1981
he was born on 12th August, 1981

casaram-se no dia 17 de Setembro
they got married on 17th September

era (o dia) 1 de Dezembro
it was the 1st December

era o Primeiro de Janeiro
it was New Year's Day (1st January)

a festa será no dia 21 de Maio
the party will be on the 21st May

C. AGE

Use **ter** (to have) + **anos** = to be X years old

quantos anos tem?
how old are you?

tenho 15 (anos)
I am 15 (years old)

quantos anos tinha...?
how old were you...?

tinha 10 anos...
I was 10...

quando fazes anos?
when is it your birthday?

quando é o seu aniversário?
when is it your birthday?

faço anos no dia 10
it's my birthday on the 10th

o meu aniversário é no 5 de Junho
my birthday is on the 5th June

fez anos ontem
he had his birthday yesterday

ela vai fazer anos amanhã
it's her birthday tomorrow

fiz 25 anos
I was 25

fará 50 anos
he will be 50

D. USEFUL EXPRESSIONS

a) Divisions of Time

o segundo	second
o minuto	minute
a hora	hour
um quarto de hora	quarter-hour
(uma) meia hora	half-hour
a manhã	morning
a tarde	afternoon
a noite	night
o dia	day
o meio-dia	midday
a meia-noite	midnight
a semana	week
quinze dias	fortnight
o mês	month
o ano	year
o século	century
o milénio	millennium

b) Expressions of Time

agora	now
agora mesmo	right now
já	right now/already

hoje	today
esta noite	tonight
ontem à noite	last night
anteontem à noite	the night before last
amanhã	tomorrow
depois de amanhã	the day after tomorrow
de/da madrugada	early in the morning
de/da manhã	in the morning
de/da tarde	in the afternoon/evening
à/da noite	at night
amanhã de manhã	tomorrow morning
ao amanhecer	at daybreak
ontem	yesterday
anteontem	the day before yesterday
a semana passada	last week
a semana que vem	next week
a semana próxima	next week
o mês passado	last month
a quinta passada	last Thursday
o domingo que vem	next Sunday
todo o dia/o dia todo	all day
ao anoitecer	at nightfall
todos os dias	every day
[BP todo dia]	
cada dia	every day
todo (o) tempo	all the time
ontem à tarde	yesterday afternoon
daqui a (uma semana)	in a (week's) time
há (dois anos)	(two years) ago

ao/no princípio do mês
at the beginning of the month

ao/no meio da semana
in the middle of the week

ao fim (no fim/no final) do ano
at the end of the year

nos anos 50
in the 50s

em 2004
in 2004

no século 21
in the twenty first century

passar tempo
to spend time

perder tempo
to waste time

uma semana de cinco dias
a five-day week

quinzenal
fortnightly

um ano bissexto
leap year

um ano civil
calendar year

um ano escolar/lectivo
school year

um ano-luz
light year

13. PREFIXES AND SUFFIXES

A. PREFIXES

Prefixes are small elements added on to the beginning of a word which change its basic meaning. The most common prefixes in Portuguese are as follows:

a) **a-/an-** = not having something/lacking

anormal	abnormal
analfabetismo	illiteracy

b) **co-/com-/con-** = joining/with

coexistir	to co-exist
compartilhar	to share
concordar	to agree

c) **de-/des-** = opposite/contrary action

decrescente	decreasing
desfazer	to undo

d) **e-/em-/en-, i-/im-/in-** = inwards movement

encarar	to face
imigrar	to immigrate
importar	to import

e) **e-/em-/en- also** = a change of state involved

embebedar	to get drunk
engordar	to get fat
evaporar	to evaporate

f) **e-/ex-** = movement away

emigrar	to emigrate
empurrar	to push
expelir	to expel

g) **i-/im-/in-/ir-** = negative

ilegítimo	illegitimate
imperfeito	imperfect
infeliz	unhappy
irresponsável	irresponsible

h) **per-** = movement through or by

percurso	route/journey
perdurar	to last a long time
perene	everlasting/perennial

i) **pre-** = prior/previous

precaução	precaution
preceder	to precede
previsão do tempo	weather forecast

j) **re-** = repetition/movement in opposite direction

reabertura	re-opening
reagir	to react
reciclar	to recycle

Others include:

i) **inter-** between/in the middle

internacional	international
interromper	to interrupt
interplanetário	interplanetary

ii) **ultra-** beyond/intensity

ultramar	overseas
ultrapassar	to overtake
ultra-som	ultrasound

iii) **ant(i)-** opposite/contrary

antipatia	antipathy
antisséptico	antiseptic
antagonista	antagonist

iv) **hipo-** inferior position/relating to horses (Greek origin)

hipocrasia	hypocrisy
hipodérmico	hypodermic
hipódromo	racecourse

v) **sin-/sim-/si-** reunion/simultaneous actions

sincronizar	to synchronize
simpatia	sympathy
sistema	system

B. SUFFIXES

Suffixes are small additions to the end of words that give those words additional meaning. They can indicate larger or smaller size, change adjectives and verbs into nouns, and transform one noun into others. The commonest suffixes are **-mente** (for adverbs), **-inho**, **-zinho**, **-zito**, **-ão**, **-zarrão**, **-ona**, **-zada** and **-zeiro**.

a) General Formation

If a word ends in a consonant, the suffix is added to the full word form, unless the word ends in **-m**, **-ão** or **-l** and is used with a suffix beginning with **z**. In this case, **-m** becomes **-n**. Plural forms drop the final **-s** before the suffix.

a manhã	morning
a manhãzinha	early morning
os pães	loaves of bread
os pãezinhos	rolls

b) Diminutives

Diminutives (**-(z)inho**, **-(z)ito**, **-isco**, **-ino**) are used to describe a person or object as small or cute, and can denote affection.

Words ending in unstressed **-o** or **-a** lose that ending and add on **-inho** or **inha**. Other words usually add **-zinho** or **-zinha**. Some others you will pick up as you go along.

a casa	house	**a casinha**	little house
a mãe	mother	**a mãezinha**	dear mother
o José	José	**o Zé/Zézinho**	little José
o gato	cat	**o gatinho**	kitten
um pouco	a little	**um pouquinho**	a tiny little bit
a filha	daughter	**a filhinha**	young/little girl, dear daughter
o rapaz	lad, boy	**o rapazinho**	little lad
pequeno	small	**pequenino**	tiny
obrigado	thank you	**obrigadinho**	thanks
pobre	poor	**pobrezinho**	poor little thing
um chá	tea	**um chazinho**	a nice little cup of tea

c) Augmentatives

Augmentatives (**-ão**, **-zarrão**, **-ona**, **-oso**) are used to describe a person or object as large, strong or ugly, and can be pejorative. In the case of **-ão**, it is added onto words ending in a consonant, and replaces the final letter of most words ending in vowels. Feminine nouns become masculine in the **-ão** augmentative. **-zarrão** follows the rules for suffixes beginning with **-z**. **-ona** is used for words describing girls and women.

a carta	letter	**o cartão**	card, cardboard
a garrafa	bottle	**o garrafão**	demijohn
a solteira	single woman	**a solteirona**	spinster
a porta	door	**o portão**	gate
a sala	room	**o salão**	large room
o gato	cat	**o gatão**	big cat
um pimento	pepper	**um pimentão**	a pepper
a palavra	word	**o palavrão**	swear word
a janela	window	**o janelão**	big (ornamental) window

C. OTHER COMMON SUFFIXES

a) **-ada**, **-ado** "-ful", group of/abundance

o papel	paper	**a papelada**	paperwork/piles of paper
a colher	spoon	**a colherada**	spoonful
o punho	fist	**o punhado**	handful
o ninho	nest	**a ninhada**	brood
a noite	night	**a noitada**	long night (out)
a criança	child	**a criançada**	group of children

b) **-ria**, **-aria** indicates place where an article is made or sold

a fruta	fruit	**a frutaria**	fruit shop/stall
o tabaco	tobacco	**a tabacaria**	tobacconist's
o pão	bread	**a padaria**	bakery

o papel	paper	**a papelaria**	stationer's
o sapato	shoe	**a sapataria**	shoeshop
o leite	milk	**a leitaria**	dairy
o peixe	fish	**a peixaria**	fishmonger's
o livro	book	**a livraria**	bookshop
o pastel	pastry/cake	**a pastelaria**	cakeshop
as jóias	jewels	**a joalharia**	jeweller's

c) **-eiro** or **-eira** indicates the tree a fruit or plant has come from

a maçã	apple	**a macieira**	apple tree
a amêndoa	almond	**a amendoeira**	almond tree
o limão	lemon	**o limoeiro**	lemon tree
o figo	fig	**a figueira**	fig tree
a rosa	rose	**a roseira**	rose tree
a laranja	orange	**a laranjeira**	orange tree
a banana	banana	**a bananeira**	banana plant
a castanha	chestnut	**o castanheiro**	chestnut tree
a noz	(wal)nut	**a nogueira**	nut tree
o damasco	apricot	**o damas-queiro**	apricot tree
a cereja	cherry	**a cerejeira**	cherry tree
o pêssego	peach	**o pessegueiro**	peach tree
a pêra	pear	**a pereira**	pear tree
a ameixa	plum	**a ameixoeira**	plum tree

d) **-ez/a**, **-ura**, **-dade**, **-ância**, **-ência**, **-dão** change adjectives into nouns, usually abstract

belo	beautiful	**beleza**	beauty
branco	white	**brancura**	whiteness
feliz	happy	**felicidade**	happiness
elegante	elegant	**elegância**	elegance
violento	violent	**violência**	violence
lento	slow	**lentidão**	slowness

e) -dor/a changes a verb into the person performing the action when added to the infinitive of a verb, after dropping the final **-r**

vender	to sell	**vendedor/a**	sales person
navegar	to navigate	**navegador/a**	sailor/navigator
trabalhar	to work	**trabalhador/a**	worker
desenhar	to design	**desenhador/a**	designer
pescar	to fish	**pescador/a**	fisherman/woman
cobrar	to charge	**cobrador/a**	money collector/conductor

f) -ante indicates an agent of an action, and also professions

calmante	calming (effect)/tranquilizer
estudante	student
tratante	form of treatment
almirante	admiral
comandante	commander
despachante	clerical agent

g) -ário/a indicates a profession, place where related items are kept, a collection of items, and qualities or states

bibliotecário	librarian
empresário	business person
operário	worker
secretário	secretary
herbário	herb garden
vestiário	dressing room/cloakroom
ovário	ovary
vocabulário	vocabulary
contrário	contrary
imaginário	imaginary
solitário	solitary
voluntário	voluntary/volunteer

h) -ês indicates origin or quality

francês French	**inglês** English	**português** Portuguese
cortês polite	**burguês** middle-class	

It also used to indicate family links

Álvares	son of	**Álvaro**
Antunes	son of	**António**
Nunes	son of	**Nuno**
Ramires	son of	**Ramiro**

i) -ista indicates followers of doctrines; professions or origins

realista	realist
modernista	modernist
budista	Buddhist
calvinista	Calvinist
dentista	dentist
jornalista	reporter
artista	artist
pianista	pianist
sulista	southerner
paulista [BP]	someone from São Paulo

D. SIMILARITY WITH ENGLISH

Certain beginnings and endings can be related to English words, such as:

a) Words ending in **-ção**

Most are equivalent to words in English ending in -tion

a estação	station

a infecção infection

More examples:

cooperação, protecção, poluição, promoção, comunicação, solução, emoção, decoração

They are all feminine words, and the plural is formed by changing the **-ção** to **-ções**:

infecções

Similarly, words ending in **-são** correspond to -sion in English

extensão extension
profissão profession
televisão television

b) There are many words starting with **es-** in Portuguese. If you remove the first **e**, you are often much closer to the English word:

escola > **scola** > school
estação > **stação** > station
espanha > **spanha** > Spain
especial > **special** > special
espaço > **spaço** > space
escala > **scala** > scale

c) Most words in Portuguese ending in **-dade** correspond to the English ending -ity:

ansiedade > anxiety
capacidade > capacity
caridade > charity
cidade > city
claridade > clarity
crueldade > cruelty
electricidade > electricity
faculdade > faculty

felicidade > felicity = happiness
integridade > integrity
luminosidade > luminosity (light)
nacionalidade > nationality
qualidade > quality
realidade > reality
variedade > variety

They are all feminine nouns in Portuguese.

d) Words ending in **-ável** in Portuguese usually correspond to -able in English. Similarly, the ending **-ível** corresponds to -ible:

admirável admirable
audível audible
comestível edible
(**comer** = to eat in Portuguese)
considerável considerable
legível legible
miserável miserable
razoável reasonable
respeitável respectable
responsável responsible
solúvel soluble
suscetível susceptible/sensitive
vulnerável vulnerable

14. IDIOMATIC EXPRESSIONS

Some expressions simply cannot be directly translated from one language to another. If an equivalent idiom cannot be found, you need to translate around the phrase. Here is a selection of idiomatic expressions.

abaixo o governo!	down with the government!
andar a cavalo	to ride a horse
andar de rasto(s)	to be worn out (physical/mental)
andar na escola/na universidade	to go to school/university
baile de fantasia	fancy dress ball
bater boca	to argue
bater com o nariz na porta	to bang one's head against the wall
um beco sem saída	a dead-end street
bradar no deserto	to protest in vain
caber a	to fall to
cá entre nós	just between us
uma carga de água	a downpour
chorar lágrimas de sangue	to cry bitterly
coisa de nada	an insignificance
coisas da vida	life's ups and downs
dar a entender	to make understand
dar certo	to turn out right/OK
dar/fazer jeito	to be useful
dar para	to look out onto
não deu por isso	he/she did not realise it
dar à luz	to give birth
dar pela coisa	to discover something
de jeito nenhum/algum!	no way!
e daí?	so what?
é isso mesmo	that's it exactly

estar a fim de	to fancy doing
estar à cunha	to be packed (eg theatre)
estar de boa/má maré	to be in a good/bad mood
estar em maus lençois	to be in a fix
estar/andar na lua	to have one's head in the clouds
falar para o boneco	to talk in vain
falar pelos cotovelos	to talk a lot
fazer asneira	to do something stupid
fazer cerimônia [BP]	to stand on ceremony
fazer chorar as pedras	to be very moving
fazer-se de bobo	to play dumb
ferver em pouca água	to worry over nothing
ficar bem	to suit
fica entre nós	this is between us
fica para (a semana)	leave it 'til (next week)
um golpe de mestre	a master stroke
haja o que houver	come what may
hoje em dia	nowadays
imagine só!	just imagine!
indas e vindas	comings and goings
ir aos arames	to get in a rage
ir mal de saúde	to be in poor health
ir ter com	to go to meet
ler nas entrelinhas	to read between the lines
levar a cabo	to carry out
um mar de rosas	a bed of roses
meter a mão em	to steal
meter o nariz (onde não é chamado)	to stick one's nose in
nada feito	nothing doing
na hora H	at the right time
nunca mais	never again
padrão de vida	standard of living
(não) passar pela cabeça	to (not) even think about

poder contar-se pelos dedos	to be able to count on one hand
pôr a mesa	to set the table
o pôr do sol	sunset
o que tem?	what's up/what's the matter?
quem diria!	who would have thought!
quem me dera!	if only (I wish I could)
saber de cor	to know by heart
se calhar	perhaps
seja como for	be that as it may
sem querer	unintentionally
se quiser	if you like
um rato de biblioteca	a bookworm
tem cada um!	it takes all sorts!
ter dois dedos na testa	to be clever
uma tempestade num copo de água	a storm in a teacup
ter a bondade de	to be so kind as to
ter a cabeça no seu lugar	to have one's head screwed on right
ter cabeça de alho chocho	to be not very clever/ distracted
ter galo	to be unlucky
ter jeito para	to have the skill for/be good at
ter razão	to be right
ter saudades de	to miss, to feel nostalgia for
vai-não-vai	wishy-washiness
vamos embora	let's be off
vista de olhos (dar uma)	(to have a) quick look
voltar à vaca fria	to return to the same matter/ subject

False friends

Some words in one language may look very similar in another, but may have a completely different meaning, and lead you into difficulty. Here are some examples:

actualmente	nowadays
assistir	to attend/be present at
bravo	wild
casualidade	chance
compromisso	appointment, meeting
concurso	contest/competition
constipado	cold
copo	glass
desgosto	displeasure/sorrow
pretender	to want, wish, intend

NDEX